1850

Fauquier County, Virginia

Slave Schedule

Patricia B. Duncan

HERITAGE BOOKS
2023

HERITAGE BOOKS

AN IMPRINT OF HERITAGE BOOKS, INC.

Books, CDs, and more—Worldwide

For our listing of thousands of titles see our website
at
www.HeritageBooks.com

Published 2023 by
HERITAGE BOOKS, INC.
Publishing Division
5810 Ruatan Street
Berwyn Heights, MD 20740

International Standard Book Number
Paperbound: 978-1-58549-819-2

INTRODUCTION

The following is a transcription of the Fauquier County, Virginia population schedule of the seventh census of the United States, 1850, Second Series, Slave Population. This census appears on National Archives microfilm No. 432, roll 986.

Handwritten numbers appear on the upper portion of some pages, but these numbers are not consistent. I therefore chose to number the pages in the order they appear.

The Ashby District, enumerator E. M. Anderson, appears on page 01 (handwritten 716) through page 63 (handwritten 841). The exceptions are pages 02 and 03 which are indicated as in the Turner District, and probably appear after the entry for Luke Woodward on my page 65. Warrenton is indicated as beginning on page 55 with the entry for Daniel Anderson, and ending on page 59 with the last entry of Col. Wm. F. Phillips. Slaves in each household are numbered consecutively in this district.

The Turner District, enumerator W. H. Rector, appears on page 64 (handwritten 844) through page 126. See above notation concerning additional pages. Slaves in each household are all numbered one in this district.

Each page that follows contains two columns of entries. Each of these columns consists of the following information:

- Name of slave owner
- Page number [see notation above]
- Number of slave [see notations above]
- Age
- Sex
- Color
- Fugitive from the State
- Number manumitted
- Deaf & dumb, blind, insane or idiotic

Sex is listed as female (f) or male (m). Color is listed as black (b) or mulatto (m). These represent skin tone, not ethnic heritage.

Although most pages are clear, some pages have been filmed with dark areas at the bottom of the page which makes transcription accuracy difficult.

1850 Fauquier Co VA Slave Schedule

CORMER, Robt.

01	01	30	m	b
01	02	16	m	b

BOWIE, Newton S.

01	01	30	f	b
01	02	13	f	b
01	03	6	f	b
01	04	3	m	b
01	05	1	f	b

BRADFORD, William

01	01	25	f	b
01	02	20	m	b

LITTLETON, Richard H.

01	01	65	f	b
01	02	24	f	m
01	03	7	f	m
01	04	4	m	b
01	05	2	f	b
01	06	10/12	m	m

PALMER, Thompson

01	01	23	m	b
01	02	22	m	b

WALLACE, George T.

01	01	12	f	b

BARBER, Thomas

01	01	30	m	b
01	02	21	m	m
01	03	15	f	b

CARTER, Catherine

01	01	45	f	b
01	02	30	m	b
01	03	17	m	m
01	04	15	f	b

ARMSTEAD, Ann

01	01	45	f	m
01	02	24	m	b
01	03	8	m	m
01	04	6	m	m

TALIAFERO, William T. W.

01	01	46	f	b
01	02	40	f	b
01	03	35	m	b
01	04	35	m	b
01	05	30	m	b
01	06	18	m	b
01	07	15	m	b
01	08	7	m	b
01	09	4	m	b
01	10	12	m	b
01	11	10	m	b
01	12	8	m	b
01	13	28	f	b
01	14	26	f	b
01	15	12	f	b
01	16	15	f	b
01	17	13	f	b
01	18	7	f	b
01	19	6	f	b
01	20	2/12	f	b
01	21	3/12	f	m

GIBSON, Sarah

01	01	50	m	b
01	02	45	m	b
01	03	50	m	b
01	04	12	m	b
01	05	10	m	b
01	06	74	f	b
01	07	60	f	b
01	08	40	f	b
01	09	40	f	b
01	10	40	f	b
01	11	30	f	b
01	12	24	f	b
01	13	32	f	b
01	14	10	f	b
01	15	9	m	b
01	16	7	m	b
01	17	4	f	b
01	18	8/12	m	b
01	19	5	m	m
01	20	4	f	m
01	21	2	m	b
01	22	6	f	b
01	23	4	f	b
01	24	2/12	m	b
01	25	8	m	m
01	26	5/12	m	m
01	27	6	m	m
01	28	6/12	m	b
01	29	14	m	b
01	30	12	f	b
01	31	12	f	b

01 32 8 m b *
* idiotic
01 33 7 m b

SAFFELL, Obed
01 01 32 f m
[see introduction]
02 01 8/12 f b

PIERCE, Manly
02 01 50 m b
02 01 25 m b
02 01 22 f b
02 01 6 f b

SMITH, Jacculin
02 01 63 m b
02 01 63 m b
02 01 30 m b
02 01 25 m b
02 01 19 m b
02 01 11 m b
02 01 3 m b
02 01 60 f b
02 01 60 f b
02 01 40 f b
02 01 33 f b
02 01 19 f b
02 01 14 f b
02 01 18 f b
02 01 7 f b
02 01 6 f b
02 01 2 f b
02 01 4/12 f b
02 01 3/12 f b
02 01 50 f b
02 01 11 f b

SUTTON, Wm. L.
02 01 28 f b
02 01 11 f b
02 01 8 f b
02 01 6 m b
02 01 19 m m
02 01 16 m b
02 01 16 m b
02 01 26 m m

PIERCE, Amos
02 01 45 f m
02 01 10 m b
02 01 30 m b
02 01 23 m b

JEFFRIES, John B.
02 01 40 m b
02 01 25 m b
02 01 25 m b
02 01 18 f b
02 01 19 f b
02 01 20 f b
02 01 11 m b
02 01 10 m b
02 01 6 m b
02 01 6 m b
02 01 4 f b
02 01 2 m b
02 01 2 m b
02 01 1 m b

RAWLINGS, John D.
02 01 35 f b
02 01 22 m m
02 01 16 m b *
* deaf & dumb
02 01 16 m b
02 01 11 m b
02 01 6 f b
02 01 4 f b
02 01 2 m b
02 01 11/12 f b

RECTOR, Thomas A.
02 01 90 f b
02 01 70 f b
02 01 46 f b
02 01 42 f b
02 01 29 f b
02 01 23 f m
02 01 23 f b
02 01 20 f b
02 01 13 f b
02 01 3 f b
02 01 3 f b
02 01 58 m b
02 01 48 m b
02 01 39 m b
02 01 25 m b
02 01 30 m b
02 01 7 m b
02 01 7 m b
02 01 4 m b
03 01 5 m b
03 01 5 m b

03 01 4 m b
03 01 1 m b
03 01 1 m m
PIERSON, Wm.
03 01 17 f b
03 01 8 m b
WITHERS, James
03 01 40 m b
03 01 25 m b
03 01 25 m b
03 01 25 m b
03 01 25 m b
03 01 15 m b
03 01 35 f b
03 01 35 f b
03 01 13 f b
03 01 11 f b
03 01 11 f b
03 01 3 f b
03 01 7/12 f b
LACEY, Benjn. R.
03 01 40 f b
03 01 35 m b
03 01 32 m b
03 01 15 m b
03 01 10 m b
03 01 15 f b
03 01 9 f b
03 01 7 f m
03 01 5 f m
RUST, Richard
03 01 35 m b
03 01 25 m m
03 01 27 f b
03 01 23 f b
03 01 13 m b
03 01 13 m b
03 01 9 f b
03 01 1 m m
BANN, Herod H.
03 01 38 m b
03 01 18 m b
03 01 10 m b
MAIDEN, Joseph
03 01 53 f b
CARR, John
03 01 30 f b
03 01 30 f b
03 01 18 f b
03 01 14 f b
03 01 36 m b
03 01 35 m b
03 01 30 m b
03 01 30 m b
03 01 30 m b
03 01 30 m b
03 01 16 m b
03 01 13 m b
03 01 12 m b
03 01 4 m b
CARTER, Westwood M.
03 01 16 f b
03 01 14 f b
03 01 6/12 m m
DULANY, Charles
03 01 31 f b
03 01 10 f b
03 01 4 m b
03 01 10/12 m b
WILSON, Sydnor
03 01 35 f b
03 01 12 m b
03 01 5 f b
03 01 3 f b
ARMISTEAD, Elizabeth
03 01 54 f b
03 01 45 f b
03 01 36 f b
03 01 32 m b
03 01 10 m b
03 01 7 m b
03 01 5 f b
03 01 1 f b
03 01 54 f b
03 01 40 f m
03 01 14 f b
03 01 12 f b
SEATON, John
03 01 90 m b
03 01 91 f b
[see introduction]
04 02 7 f m
04 03 6 m m
04 04 1 f b
THOMPSON, William
04 01 50 f b

04 02 12 m b
CORDER, James
04 01 15 f b
RUSSEL, Wesley
04 01 30 f b
04 02 12 f b
04 03 10 m b
04 04 3 f b
BOLEN, Jessee
04 01 54 f b
04 02 55 m b
04 03 10 m b
04 04 11 f b
04 05 4 f b
FERGGUSON, Elizabeth
04 01 32 f m
04 02 10/12 f m
04 03 30 f b
FERGGUSON, Jno. D.
04 01 35 m b
04 02 48 m b
04 03 25 f b
04 04 17 f b
04 05 13 m b
04 06 5 f b
04 07 7 m b
04 08 2 m b
FERGGUSON, Harriett
04 01 10 f b
04 02 4 f b
FERGGUSON, James
04 01 40 m m
04 02 26 m b
04 03 20 m b
04 04 24 m b
04 05 18 m b
04 06 30 f m
04 07 26 f b
04 08 16 f m
04 09 13 f b
04 10 10 f b
04 11 6 m b
04 12 5 m b
04 13 4 m b *
* idiotic
04 14 2 m b
04 15 6/12 f m
PEER, Catharine
04 01 40 m b
NALLEY, Jessee
04 01 75 m b
04 02 70 m b
04 03 35 m b
04 04 40 m b
04 05 36 f b
04 06 25 m b
04 07 20 m b
04 08 6 m b
04 09 4 m b
04 10 13 f b
STROTHER, Jno.
04 01 43 m b
04 02 40 m b
04 03 28 m m
04 04 25 f b
04 05 22 m b
04 06 19 m b
04 07 14 m b
04 08 12 f b
04 09 10 f b
04 10 5 f b
04 11 2 m b
COLSTON, Raleigh
04 01 44 m b
04 02 40 m b
04 03 30 m b
04 04 29 m m
04 05 23 m b
04 06 19 m m
04 07 48 f b
04 08 29 f m
04 09 20 f m
04 10 20 f b
04 11 40 f m
04 12 17 f b
04 13 14 f m
04 14 15 f m
04 15 12 f m
04 16 10 f m
04 17 11 f m
04 18 5 m b
04 19 ? m b
05 20 1 m m
05 21 1 m b
SETTLE, Abner
05 01 42 f m

05 02 40 m b
05 03 38 f m
05 04 19 f m
05 05 19 m b
05 06 7 f b
05 07 8 f m
05 08 4 m m

PIERCE, Hector
05 01 21 m m
05 02 21 m b
05 03 21 m b
05 04 35 f b
05 05 5 m b
05 06 16 m b

BRADFIELD, James
05 01 15 f b

BROWN, Jno. W.
05 01 11 f m

GREEN, Ann
05 01 50 f b
05 02 43 m b
05 03 13 f m
05 04 6 f b

RICE, James
05 01 60 f b
05 02 10 m m

CRUPPER, Jno. T.
05 01 17 f b

LATEN, Jno. D.
05 01 14 m b

PENQUITE, Joseph
05 01 36 f b
05 02 5 m m

BIRD, William G.
05 01 47 f b
05 02 3 f b

WATKINS, George
05 01 13 f b

RUST, James
05 01 68 f b
05 02 52 f b
05 03 50 f b
05 04 27 m b
05 05 22 f b
05 06 19 m b
05 07 19 m b
05 08 19 m b
05 09 43 m b
05 10 9 f b
05 11 6 m b
05 12 5 m b
05 13 4 m b
05 14 2 m b
05 15 2 f b
05 16 2/12 f b
05 17 21 f b *
* idiotic
05 18 8 m b

OREAR, Enoch
05 01 42 m b
05 02 35 m b
05 03 25 m b
05 04 22 m b
05 05 17 f b
05 06 7 f b
05 07 5 f b
05 08 6/12 f b
05 09 45 f b
05 10 18 f b
05 11 13 m b

PAYNE, Doct. A.
05 01 35 f b
05 02 15 m b
05 03 4 m b
05 04 2 f b
05 05 3/12 m b
05 06 3/12 m b

ROGERS, Wm. W.
05 01 12 m b
05 02 12 f b

KERCHEVALL, Willas
05 01 17 m m
05 02 12 f m

CRUPPER, Eli
05 01 50 m b
05 02 40 m b
05 03 16 f b
05 04 23 m b
05 05 12 m b

ASHBY, Thompson
05 01 24 f b
05 02 22 f b
05 03 19 m b
05 04 17 m m
05 05 9 f m
05 06 10 f b

05 07 6/12 m m
McQUINN, Luntzford
05 01 7 f b
SHERMAN, Thomas
05 01 40 m b
06 02 28 m m
06 03 26 m m
06 04 21 m m
06 05 15 m m
06 06 13 m m
06 07 15 f b
06 08 15 f b
06 09 26 f m
06 10 10 f m
06 11 8 f m
06 12 6 f m
06 13 5 m b
06 14 5 m b
06 15 2 f b
06 16 1 m b
06 17 1 m b
06 18 2 f m
06 19 2 m m
ASHBY, William
06 01 48 m b
06 02 19 m b
06 03 15 m b
BROOK, Jno. L.
06 01 42 f b
06 02 40 f b
06 03 20 m b
06 04 16 f m
06 05 12 m b
06 06 10 m b
06 07 10 m b
06 08 10 f b
06 09 8 f b
06 10 4 m b
06 11 4 f b
06 12 2 f b
06 13 2 f b
06 14 4/12 f b
EDMONDS, Lewis
06 01 85 f b
06 02 60 f b
06 03 70 m b
06 04 38 m m
06 05 25 f b
06 06 22 f b
06 07 16 m b
06 08 13 m b
06 09 12 m b
06 10 45 m b
06 11 7 m b
06 12 5 m b
06 13 3 m b
06 14 2 m b
06 15 8/12 m b
06 16 9/12 m m
TRIPLETT, Benj'a.
06 01 45 f b
06 02 32 f b
06 03 40 m b
06 04 26 m b
06 05 18 f b
06 06 28 f b
06 07 15 f b
06 08 12 m b
06 09 9 m b
06 10 7 m b
06 11 2 f b
06 12 6/12 m b
06 13 6/12 m b
06 14 6/12 m b
SAFFELL, Obed
06 01 17 f b
BROWN, James
06 01 70 m b
06 02 16 f b
BROWN, Archable
06 01 25 f m
06 02 15 m b
06 03 9 m m
06 04 8 f m
06 05 5 f m
06 06 3 f m
06 07 60 m b
CORNWELL, Jacob
06 01 50 f b
06 02 30 m b
06 03 30 m b
06 04 30 m b
06 05 26 f b
06 06 27 f b
06 07 12 f b
06 08 4? f b

07 09 4 f m
07 10 8 m m
07 11 8 m m
07 12 8 m m
07 13 5 m b
07 14 3 f b
07 15 7/12 m m
07 16 1 f m

CORDER, Joseph
07 01 60 m b

FERGGUSON, Jno. D.
07 01 62 f b
07 02 62 m b
07 03 25 m b
07 04 18 m m
07 05 15 m m
07 06 13 f m

McDANIEL, Thomas
07 01 48 f b
07 02 12 m b

IDEN, Manly
07 01 40 f b
07 02 30 m m
07 03 6 f b

BOARD, Thomas C.
07 01 43 f b
07 02 8 m b
07 03 6 m b
07 04 2 f b
07 05 1 f b

ANDERSON, Eli
07 01 65 m b
07 02 52 m b
07 03 46 m b
07 04 46 f b
07 05 33 f b
07 06 31 m b
07 07 27 m b
07 08 29 f b
07 09 25 m b
07 10 23 m b
07 11 21 f b
07 12 17 m m
07 13 12 f b
07 14 14 m b
07 15 12 m b
07 16 8 f b
07 17 4 f b
07 18 4 f b
07 19 10 m b
07 20 8 m b
07 21 6 f b
07 22 3 m b
07 23 1 m b
07 24 2 f b
07 25 10/12 f b

BOWIE, Jno.
07 01 50 m b
07 02 57 f b
07 03 16 f b
07 04 8 f b
07 05 4 f b
07 06 9/12 m b

ROGERS, Notly W.
07 01 121 f m

SHORT, Thomas
07 01 65 m b
07 02 65 m b
07 03 55 m b
07 04 12 m b
07 05 12 f b

TURNER, William
07 01 36 f m
07 02 5 m b
07 03 3 f b

WINES, James M.
07 01 25 m b
07 02 19 m b
07 03 19 f b

ADAMS, Sarah
07 01 48 m b
07 02 37 f b
07 03 26 f b
07 04 25 f b
07 05 24 m b
07 06 14 m b
07 07 7 m b

KEITH, Alexander D.
07 01 73 f b
07 02 64 m b
07 03 64 m b
07 04 40 m b
07 05 35 f b
07 06 14 m b
07 07 6 m b
07 08 1 f b

07 09 1 f b
DAWSON, Jno. A.
08 01 34 f b
08 02 11 m b
08 03 9 f b
EVANS, Samuel
08 01 11 f b
BRADFORD, Benj'a. R.
08 01 80 f b
08 02 80 m m
08 03 76 f b
08 04 39 m b
08 05 17 f b
08 06 32 f m
08 07 13 m m
08 08 11 f m
08 09 10 f m
08 10 8 f m
08 11 1 m m
THOMPSON, Landa
08 01 30 f b
08 02 10 m b
08 03 12 f m
08 04 5 m m
08 05 4 m m
08 06 1 m m
GREEN, A. G.
08 01 30 f m
08 02 4 m m
HERRELL, Jno.
08 01 55 f b
08 02 7 m b
08 03 3 m b
08 04 4/12 f b
FEAGANS, Hannah
08 01 60 f b
08 02 28 f m
08 03 26 f b
08 04 16 m b
08 05 9 m m
08 06 9 m m
08 07 8 m m
08 08 6 f b
08 09 6 f m
08 10 4 m m
08 11 2 m b
08 12 2 f b
08 13 1 f m
FEAGANS, Daniel
08 01 45 f b
08 02 23 m b
08 03 18 m b
08 04 14 m b
08 05 13 f m
08 06 10 f b
08 07 8 f b
08 08 4 f b
08 09 2 m m
08 10 1 m m
LAWS, Newman
08 01 50 f b
08 02 50 f b
08 03 50 m b
08 04 20 m b
08 05 30 m b
08 06 6 m b
LAWS, Shadrick
08 01 28 m b
08 02 23 f b
08 03 22 m b
08 04 20 f b
08 05 5 m b
08 06 1 m b
GRIGSBY, Mary
08 01 70 f b
08 02 65 f m
08 03 45 f b
08 04 40 f m
08 05 40 m b
08 06 26 m b
08 07 22 f m
08 08 8 m b
08 09 6 f m
08 10 2 m m
08 11 7/12 f m
08 12 50 m m
ASHBY, Alcinda
08 01 52 f b
08 02 8 f b
08 03 6 m b
08 04 4 f b
08 05 2 f b
HARTMAN, Peter
08 01 50 m b
08 02 38 m b
08 03 20 m b

08 04 73 m b
08 05 28? m b
09 06 6 m b
09 07 4 m b
09 08 33 f b
09 09 30 f b
09 10 16 f b
09 11 9 f b
09 12 8 f b
09 13 7 f b
09 14 1 f b
09 15 2 f b
09 16 8/12 f b

STROTHER, James W.
09 01 13 f m

FRED, Joseph
09 01 55 f b
09 02 40 f b
09 03 45 m b
09 04 19 m b
09 05 9 m b

CHINN, Andrews
09 01 75 m m
09 02 75 m m
09 03 60 m b
09 04 40 m b
09 05 35 m b
09 06 25 m m
09 07 25 m m
09 08 26 m b
09 09 60 f b
09 10 50 f m
09 11 36 f m
09 12 25 f b
09 13 10 f m
09 14 8 f m
09 15 6 f m
09 16 4 f m
09 17 1 m m
09 18 6 f b
09 19 1 f b
09 20 12 m b
09 21 10 f m

ROSTIN, Joseph A.
09 01 11 f b
09 02 7 m b

HERENDON, Revd. Thadius
09 01 42 m m
09 02 30 m b
09 03 33 f m
09 04 15 f m
09 05 13 m m
09 06 11 m m
09 07 11 f m
09 08 8 m m
09 09 7 f m
09 10 5 f m
09 11 1 m m

OREAR, Jessee
09 01 14 f b
09 02 12 m b

ADAMS, Benj'a. F.
09 01 50 m m
09 02 30 f m
09 03 7 f b

PIERCE, Ansell J.
09 01 38 m b
09 02 16 m b
09 03 25 f b
09 04 12 f b

ASHBY, Jno. J.
09 01 90 f m
09 02 60 f b
09 03 60 m b
09 04 49 m b
09 05 40 m b
09 06 35 f b
09 07 22 m b
09 08 21 m b
09 09 20 m m
09 10 16 m b
09 11 14 f b
09 12 5 f b

JACKSON, George
09 01 25 m b
09 02 25 m b
09 03 23 f b
09 04 9 f b
09 05 1 m b
09 06 20 f b
09 07 14 m m

ASHBY, Lucy
09 01 70 f b
09 02 30 m b
09 03 25 f b
09 04 18 f b

09 05 9 m b
10 06 10 f b
10 07 2 f b
10 08 1 f b

GIBSON, Charles
10 01 37 m b
10 02 35 m b
10 03 31 m m
10 04 15 m b
10 05 11 m b
10 06 7 m b
10 07 6 m m
10 08 4 m m
10 09 3 m b
10 10 32 f b
10 11 29 f m
10 12 9 f m
10 13 8 f m
10 14 5 f b
10 15 4/12 f b

BUTCHER, Edgar M.
10 01 70 f b *
* blind
10 02 60 m b
10 03 19 m b
10 04 13 f b
10 05 8 f b

ASH, Frances F.
10 01 16 f b
10 02 14 m b
10 03 8 m b
10 04 6 f b

ASH, Mariah
10 01 75 f b
10 02 39 f b
10 03 45 f b
10 04 23 m m
10 05 17 m m
10 06 15 m b
10 07 13 m m
10 08 13 m b
10 09 11 f m
10 10 11 m b

LONG, Robt.
10 01 14 m b
10 02 7 f b
10 03 4 f b

WISER, Henry T.
10 01 45 m b
10 02 30 m b
10 03 30 f b
10 04 15 m b
10 05 12 m m
10 06 10 f b
10 07 5 f b
10 08 1 f b
10 09 3 m b

ADAMS, Jno.
10 01 66 f b
10 02 25 m b
10 03 19 m b
10 04 9 f b

ASHBY, Elizabeth T.
10 01 78 m b
10 02 85 f b
10 03 58 f b
10 04 43 f b
10 05 40 m b
10 06 38 m b
10 07 40 f b
10 08 34 f b
10 09 16 f b
10 10 14 f b
10 11 14 f b
10 12 12 m b
10 13 8 m b
10 14 6 m b
10 15 4 f b
10 16 68 m b

SHACKLETT, Hezekiah
10 01 90 m b
10 02 60 f b
10 03 50 m b
10 04 50 m b
10 05 35 m b
10 06 35 f b
10 07 14 f m
10 08 13 m b
10 09 8 m b
10 10 3 7 b

WINES, Hedgman
10 01 10 f b

SMITH, Jno. T.
10 01 70 f b
10 02 65 m b
10 03 32 m m

10 04 23? f m
11 05 35 m b
11 06 35 m b
11 07 22 m b
11 08 18 m b
11 09 12 m b
11 10 10 f b
11 11 8 f b
11 12 6 f b
11 13 22 f b
11 14 8 f b
11 15 6 f b
11 16 4 f b
11 17 1 f b

CURLETT, Susan H.
11 01 49 m b
11 02 45 f b
11 03 42 m m
11 04 28 f m
11 05 29 m b
11 06 26 m b
11 07 24 f m
11 08 22 f m
11 09 12 m b
11 10 10 f b
11 11 10 m b
11 12 6 m b
11 13 5 m b
11 14 3 m b
11 15 1 m b
11 16 3/12 f b
11 17 5 f m
11 18 4 m b
11 19 2 m m

PHILLIPS, Thomas
11 01 48 m b
11 02 40 f b
11 03 18 f b
11 04 14 f b
11 05 1 m b

MARSHALL, F. Lewis
11 01 65 m b
11 02 55 f b
11 03 45 f b
11 04 40 f m
11 05 30 m b
11 06 30 f m
11 07 27 m m
11 08 25 m b
11 09 45 f m
11 10 23 f b
11 11 21 m b
11 12 18 m m
11 13 15 m m
11 14 14 m b
11 15 13 m m
11 16 13 f m
11 17 8 f m
11 18 6 f m
11 19 4 m m
11 20 3 f m
11 21 2 f m
11 22 1 m m
11 23 1 f m

TRASY, Lewis
11 01 50 m b
11 02 30 m b
11 03 27 f m
11 04 12 f b
11 05 5 f b

SMITH, Lucy
11 01 52 f b
11 02 45 m b
11 03 27 f b
11 04 12 f b
11 05 8 f b

MORGAN, Josaphine
11 01 25 f b
11 02 9 m b
11 03 7 f b
11 04 5 f b
11 05 2 f b

RANDOLPH, William F.
11 01 60 m b
11 02 47 f b
11 03 30 f b
11 04 8 m b
11 05 6 m b
11 06 4 f b
11 07 1 f b

PIERSON, James
11 01 16 f b

BOUSET?, Jno.
12 01 56 m b
12 02 28 f b
12 03 13 f m

PIERSON, Thomas
12 01 51 f b
12 02 22 m b
12 03 20 m b
12 04 14 f m
12 05 76 m b

BALEY, Samuel
12 01 94 f b
12 02 70 f b
12 03 60 m b
12 04 48 m b
12 05 48 m b
12 06 45 m b
12 07 30 m b
12 08 28 m b
12 09 40 f b
12 10 35 f b
12 11 28 f b
12 12 24 f b
12 13 14 m b
12 14 12 f b
12 15 12 f b
12 16 8 m b
12 17 8 m b
12 18 6 m b
12 19 6 f b
12 20 5 m m
12 21 4 m m
12 22 2 m m
12 23 7/12 m b
12 24 4 m b

MADDOX, Dauphin
12 01 42 m b
12 02 43 m b
12 03 23 m b
12 04 19 m b
12 05 16 f m
12 06 14 m m
12 07 8 f m
12 08 4 f m
12 09 4 f m

ROGERS, Hugh
12 01 45 m b
12 02 50 f b
12 03 21 m b
12 04 17 m b
12 05 18 m m
12 06 16 f m
12 07 13 f b
12 08 3 f b
12 09 1 f b

TURNER, James T.
12 01 75 m b
12 02 40 f b
12 03 55 f b
12 04 8 f b
12 05 5 m b
12 06 3 m b
12 07 47 m b

TURNER, William F.
12 01 62 m b
12 02 40 f b
12 03 18 f b
12 04 10 m b
12 05 8 m b
12 06 4 f b

RICKORY, Smith H.
12 01 34 m b
12 02 30 m b
12 03 22 f b
12 04 22 f b
12 05 22 f b
12 06 24 f b
12 07 19 f b
12 08 13 f b
12 09 8 m m
12 10 7 m b
12 11 6 f b
12 12 6 f b
12 13 4 m m
12 14 4 m b
12 15 2 m m
12 16 2/12 f b

SHACALETT, Washington
12 01 40 m b
12 02 18 f b
12 03 8 f b
12 04 4/12 f b

ROBBERSON, Joseph
13 01 23 f b
13 02 5 m m
13 03 4/12 m b

SANDERS, Frank
13 01 10 f b

HANSFORD, Andrew
13 01 44 m b

13 02 30 m b
13 03 17 f b
13 04 26 f b
13 05 24 m m
13 06 2 m b
13 07 8/12 f b
13 08 4/12 m b

ADAMS, Thomas T.

13 01 50 f b
13 02 25 m b
13 03 20 f b

BLACKMORE, James

13 01 70 m m
13 01 58 m b
13 03 36 m b
13 04 33 f b
13 05 32 f m
13 06 24 m b
13 07 20 m b
13 08 18 m b
13 09 17 m b
13 10 20 f b
13 11 15 m b
13 12 12 m b
13 13 10 f b
13 14 10 f b
13 15 9 f b
13 16 7 f b
13 17 7 f b
13 18 5 m b
13 19 4 m b
13 20 2 m b
13 21 1 f b

RUST, Fleet G.

13 01 44 m m
13 02 26 f b
13 03 24 m b
13 04 23 m b
13 05 16 f m
13 06 9 m b
13 07 7 m b
13 08 5 f b
13 09 15 m b

KERRICK, Mathew M.

13 01 12 f b

STRIBBLING, Doct. Wm.

13 01 56 m b
13 02 29 m b
13 03 24 m b
13 04 26 m b
13 05 45 m b
13 06 36 f m
13 07 75 f m
13 08 30 f b
13 09 22 f b
13 10 23 f b
13 11 23 m b
13 12 14 m b
13 13 13 f b
13 14 12 f b
13 15 8 m b
13 16 5 m b
13 17 2 f m
13 18 3 f m
13 19 1 m b
13 20 5 f b
13 21 2 f b
13 22 1 f b

PAGE, Cam T.

13 01 62 f b
13 02 50 f b
13 03 30 m b
13 04 28 f m
13 05 22 f b
13 06 23 f b
13 07 20 m b
13 08 17 m m
13 09 16 m b
13 10 16 m m
13 11 12 f b
13 12 9 f b
13 13 9 f b
13 14 7 m b
13 15 6 f m
13 16 2 f b
14 17 2 f b
14 18 1 f b
14 19 9/12 m b

ASHBY, Samuel T.

14 01 55 f b
14 02 23 f b
14 03 14 f b
14 04 13 f m
14 05 40 m b
14 06 25 m b
14 07 18 m b

14 08 33 m b
ABBOTT, Ezra
14 01 55 m b
14 02 49 f b
14 03 24 f b
14 04 17 f b
MARSHALL, Thomas G.
14 01 50 m b
14 02 40 m b
14 03 32 m b
14 04 30 m b
14 05 30 f b
14 06 30 f b
14 07 26 m b
14 08 18 m b
14 09 21 f b
14 10 14 m b
14 11 13 f b
14 12 11 m b
14 13 10 f b
14 14 8 m b
14 15 7 m b
14 16 6 f b
14 17 5 f b
14 18 4 m b
14 19 4 m b
14 20 2 m b
14 21 2 m b
14 22 2 m b
14 23 1 f b
14 24 10/12 f b
14 25 4/12 f b
14 26 7/12 m b
HALY, David
14 01 31 m b
ROLES, George W.
14 01 35 f b
14 02 15 m b
ROLES, Margarett
14 01 17 m b
14 02 12 m b
MORRIS, Manly D.
14 01 11 f b
SMITH, Mariah
14 01 25 f b
14 02 1 m b
TAYLOR, Herbert
14 01 40 f b
14 02 30 m b
14 03 25 m b
14 04 24 m b
HUDLIN, Richard
14 01 45 f b
14 02 19 m b
14 03 18 f b
14 04 14 m m
14 05 10 m b
14 06 6 f b
14 07 4/12 m b
JETT, Peter
14 01 50 f b
SMITH, Elijah
14 01 60 m b
14 02 60 f b
14 03 24 f b
14 04 22 m m
14 05 21 m m
14 06 20 m b
14 07 18 m m
14 08 17 f m
14 09 15 m m
14 10 11 m b
14 11 8 m b
14 12 1 f m
14 13 8/12 m b
14 14 3 f b
FEAGANS, Bushrod
14 01 12 m b
WATTERS, Emaly
14 01 50 f b
14 02 23 f b
14 03 9 f b
14 04 8 m b
14 05 3 m m
LEACH, William F.
14 01 27 f b
14 02 8 m b
HOLMS, Nathaniel C.
14 01 28 f m
15 02 12 f m
MADDOX, James D.
15 01 35 f m
15 02 10 m m
15 03 7 m b
15 04 4 m m
15 05 1 m m

15 06 15 m b
HUDLIN, Alexander
15 01 25 f b
15 02 13 f b
HITCH, Rachel
15 01 30 f b
15 02 40 m b
15 03 14 m m
DOWNING, Jno. H.
15 01 40 f b
15 02 35 f b
15 03 50 m b
15 04 33 m b
15 05 27 m b
15 06 23 f b
15 07 19 f m
15 08 16 m b
15 09 14 m b
15 10 12 m b
15 11 10 m b
15 12 8 f b
15 13 12 f b
15 14 8 f b
15 15 7 m b
15 16 5 f b
15 17 4 m b
15 18 3 f b
15 19 1 f b
MARSHALL, Henry M.
15 01 60 m b
15 02 60 m m
15 03 40 f b
15 04 36 f b
15 05 34 f b
15 06 25 f b
15 07 22 f b
15 08 25 f b
15 09 20 f b
15 10 20 f b
15 11 35 m b
15 12 28 m b
15 13 40 m m
15 14 20 m b
15 15 18 m b
15 16 16 m b
15 17 22 m b
15 18 20 m b
15 19 15 m b
15 20 13 m b
15 21 13 m b
15 22 36 m b
15 23 12 f b
15 24 12 f m
15 25 15 m b
15 26 8 f b
15 27 8 m b
15 28 5 f b
15 29 2 m b
15 30 8 m b
15 31 6 m b
15 32 10 m b
15 33 8 f b
15 34 6 m b
15 35 4 f b
15 36 6/12 m b
15 37 5 m b
15 38 1 f b
15 39 1 m b
15 40 6/12 f b
MADDOX, Jessee
15 01 8 f b
AMBLER, Doct. R. C.
15 01 100 m b
15 02 50 m b
15 03 45 m b
15 04 35 m b
15 05 25 m b
15 06 25 m b
15 07 25 m b
15 08 25 m b
15 09 24 m b
15 10 75 m b
15 11 70 f b
15 12 25 f b
16 13 60 f b
16 14 54 f b
16 15 40 f b
16 16 40 f b
16 17 40 f b
16 18 40 f b
16 19 44 f b
16 20 25 f b
16 21 25 f b
16 22 16 f m
16 23 10 f b
16 24 9 m b

16 25 7 f b
16 26 5 f b
16 27 3 m b
16 28 1 f b
16 29 10 m m
16 30 8 f m
16 31 7 m m
16 32 6 f m
16 33 4 f m
16 34 9 m m
16 35 7 f m
16 36 6 f m
16 37 4 m m
16 38 2 m m
16 39 9 m m

SHORT, George L.
16 01 13 f b
16 02 10 m b
16 03 8 m b
16 04 5 f b

WIGFIELD, Jno.
16 01 70 f b
16 02 53 f b
16 03 35 f m
16 04 35 m m
16 05 26 m b
16 06 16 f b
16 07 16 f b
16 08 13 f m
16 09 11 f m
16 10 9 m b
16 11 6 m b
16 12 2 m m
16 13 9/12 f m

MORRISON, Jno. A.
16 01 39 m b
16 02 12 f m
16 03 5 f b

MORRISON, Mary
16 01 34 f b
16 02 12 f b
16 03 10 f b
16 04 2 m b
16 05 4 f b
16 06 4/12 f b

WHITE, Charles
16 01 90 m b
16 02 90 f b
16 03 45 m b
16 04 45 m b
16 05 40 m b
16 06 40 m b
16 07 22 m m
16 08 20 m m
16 09 18 m m
16 10 17 m b
16 11 16 m b
16 12 12 m b
16 13 10 m m
16 14 8 m b
16 15 2 m m
16 16 40 f m
16 17 37 f b
16 18 23 f m
16 19 14 f m
16 20 10 f b
16 21 8 f b
16 22 6 f m
16 23 4 f b
16 24 1 f b
16 25 2 m b
16 26 6/12 m m
16 27 6/12 f b

PIERSON, Jno.
16 01 49 m b
16 02 26 m b
16 03 40 m m
16 04 22? m b
17 05 25 m b
17 06 20 m b
17 07 22 m b *
17 08 23 m b *

* fugitive

17 09 14 m b
17 10 11 m b
17 11 2 m b
17 12 1 m b
17 13 30 f m
17 14 30 f b
17 15 6 f b
17 16 6 f b
17 17 4 f b
17 18 3 f b

AMBLER, Thomas M.
17 01 65 f b
17 02 65 m b

17	03	49	m	b
17	04	47	m	b
17	05	36	m	b
17	06	21	m	b
17	07	63	m	b
17	08	52	m	b
17	09	42	m	b
17	10	19	m	b
17	11	12	m	b
17	12	22	m	b
17	13	16	m	b
17	14	14	m	b
17	15	8	m	b
17	16	5	m	b
17	17	1	m	b
17	18	25	m	b
17	19	26	m	b
17	20	2	m	b
17	21	6	m	b
17	22	3	m	b
17	23	57	f	b
17	24	23	f	b
17	25	7	f	b
17	26	27	f	b
17	27	12	f	m
17	28	5	f	m
17	29	3	f	b
17	30	1	f	b
17	31	24	f	b
17	32	8	f	b
17	33	6	f	b
17	34	3/12	f	b
17	35	43	f	b
17	36	26	f	b
17	37	20	f	b
17	38	1	f	b
17	39	12	f	b
17	40	10	f	b

AMBLER, Jno. M.

17	01	30	m	b
17	02	28	m	b
17	03	18	f	b
17	04	28	f	b
17	05	12	f	b
17	06	7	m	b
17	07	5	f	b
17	08	3	f	b
17	09	1	f	b

ASHBY, James

17	01	56	f	b
17	02	55	f	b
17	03	28	f	b
17	04	8	m	b
17	05	6	m	b
17	06	5	f	m
17	07	4	m	b
17	08	2	m	b
17	09	4/12	m	b

ASHBY, Turner

17	01	55	m	b
17	02	6	m	b
17	03	7	f	b

FLETCHER, Elias

17	01	27	m	b
17	02	25	m	b
17	03	16	f	b
17	04	15	m	b
17	05	12	m	m
17	06	10	m	b
17	07	10	m	b

KNIGHT, James

17	01	25	f	b
17	02	1	m	m

MOREHEAD, Armistead H.

18	01	45	f	b
18	02	35	f	b
18	03	55	f	b
18	04	35	f	b
18	05	22	m	b
18	06	22	m	b
18	07	17	m	b
18	08	12	m	b
18	09	12	m	b
18	10	11	m	b
18	11	6	f	b
18	12	5	m	b
18	13	3	m	b
18	14	3	f	b
18	15	6	f	b
18	16	3	f	b
18	17	4/12	m	b
18	18	8/12	f	b

PARSONS, William

18	01	16	f	b

COATNEY, Albert

18	01	9	f	b

WEAVER, Jacob
18 01 38 f b
18 02 18 f b
18 03 9 f m
18 04 7 m b
18 05 5 f b
18 06 3 m b
PRIEST, Lucy
18 01 10 m b
SANFORD, Lawrence
18 01 60 m b
18 02 40 m b
18 03 40 m b
18 04 35 m b
18 05 25 m b
18 06 24 m b
18 07 23 m m
18 08 22 m b
18 09 23 m b
18 10 18 m b
18 11 15 m b
18 12 62 f b
18 13 33 f b
18 14 30 f b
18 15 22 f b
18 16 17 f b
18 17 16 f b
18 18 11 m b
18 19 10 m b
18 20 6 m b
18 21 5 m b
18 22 4 f b
18 23 3 f b
18 24 1 f b
18 25 3 f b
MINTER, Jno. T.
18 01 14 m b
ADAMS, George
18 01 54 m b
18 02 54 f b
18 03 42 m b
18 04 21 m b
18 05 14 m b
18 06 12 f b
WITHERS, Doct. Thomas T.
18 01 50 f m
18 02 40 m b
18 03 35 m b
18 04 30 m m
18 05 25 f m
18 06 20 f m
18 07 8 m m
18 08 8 f m
18 09 4 f m
SCOTT, Robt.
18 01 35 f b
18 02 8 m b
18 03 4 m b
18 04 68 m b
18 05 45 f b
18 06 45 f b
18 07 40 m b
18 08 45 f b
18 09 35 f b
18 10 22 m m
18 11 18 m b
18 12 14 f b
18 13 12 m b
18 14 9 f b
18 15 3? ? b
19 16 4 m m
DICKSON, Alexander
19 01 45 f b
19 02 10 m b
19 03 8 m b
19 04 4 m b
BARBER, Joseph A.
19 01 40 f b
19 02 18 m b
19 03 16 m m
19 04 5 m b
HEATON, Benj'n. M.
19 01 37 f m
19 02 12 f b
19 03 5 f b
19 04 3 m b
19 05 9/12 f b
FEAGANS, Jno. R.
19 01 65 m b
19 02 65 f b
19 03 38 m b
19 04 38 m b
19 05 30 m b
19 06 25 m b
19 07 22 f b
19 08 16 m b

19 09 15 f b
19 10 12 f b
19 11 9 m b
19 12 15 f b
19 13 8 m b
19 14 5 f b
19 15 4 m b
19 16 3 m b

PAGE, Mary J.
19 01 22 f b
19 02 9 f b
19 03 7 f b
19 04 4 f m
19 05 8 f m

ESSEX, William
19 01 12 f m

JETT, Marshall
19 01 35 m b
19 02 10 f b

SHOEMAKER, Jno.
19 01 28 m b
19 02 26 m b
19 03 24 m b
19 04 24 m b
19 05 21 m b
19 06 20 m m
19 07 18 f m
19 08 14 f m
19 09 11 f m
19 10 9 m m
19 11 7 m m
19 12 5 f m
19 13 65 m b

RICKSEY, Benj. F.
19 01 60 m b
19 02 70 f b
19 03 50 m b
19 04 45 f b
19 05 40 m b
19 06 40 m b
19 07 25 m b
19 08 36 f b
19 09 18 m b
19 10 25 f b
19 11 20 f b
19 12 20 f b
19 13 16 m b
19 14 13 m b
19 15 12 m b
19 16 12 f b
19 17 8 m b
19 18 7 m b
19 19 5 m b
19 20 3 m b
19 21 1 m b
19 22 3 f b
19 23 2 f b
19 24 9/12 f b
19 25 9/12 m b
19 26 6/12 f b

NELSON, George A.
19 01 18 m b
19 02 18 m b
19 03 60 f b
19 04 16 f b
19 05 9 m b
19 06 7 m b

ROGERS, Stephen
20 01 25 f b
20 02 19 m b
20 03 20 m m
20 04 17 f b
20 05 1 f m

ROGERS, Gabriel
20 01 23 m b
20 02 75 m m
20 03 40 f b
20 04 15 f b
20 05 5 f b
20 06 5 f b
20 07 2 m b
20 08 1 f b

SMITH, James
20 01 80 f b
20 02 45 f b
20 03 18 f b

JETT, William
20 01 41 f b
20 02 40 f b
20 03 38 m b
20 04 36 m b
20 05 33 m b
20 06 32 m b
20 07 24 m b
20 08 16 m b
20 09 10 f b

20 10 7 m b
20 11 6 f b

PAYNE, Jno. C.

20 01 48 f b
20 02 25 m b
20 03 25 m b
20 04 20 f b
20 05 17 f b
20 06 10 m b
20 07 7 m b
20 08 7 f b
20 09 1 m b
20 10 6/12 m b

TEMPLEMAN, Edward P.

20 01 60 m b
20 02 24 m b
20 03 13 m b
20 04 22 f b
20 05 21 f b
20 06 8 f b
20 07 3 m m
20 08 1 m b
20 09 1 m b

PAYNE, Jno.

20 01 9 f b

RICHARD, Sophiah

20 01 49 f b
20 02 39 f b
20 03 10 f b
20 04 4 f b
20 05 3 f b

PAYNE, Enos

20 01 15 f b
20 02 12 f b

DANIEL, William

20 01 46 m m
20 02 40 m m
20 03 16 m m
20 04 17 f m
20 05 13 f m
20 06 10 f b
20 07 8 m b
20 08 7 f b
20 09 6 f b
20 10 5 m b
20 11 4 m b
20 12 25 m m

McQUIN, George W.

20 01 36 f b

GRIGSBY, James M.

20 01 55 m b
20 02 48 f b
20 03 40 f b
20 04 15 f b
20 05 7 m b

GLASSCOCK, William D.

20 01 71 f b
20 02 48 m b
20 03 25 m b
20 04 24 m m
20 05 21 f b
20 06 18 f m
20 07 24 f m
20 08 14 m b
20 09 12 m b
20 10 9 f b
20 11 7 f b
20 12 ? m m
21 13 1 f m

PALMER, Jno.

21 01 28 m b
21 02 26 m b
21 03 19 m b
21 04 18 f b
21 05 14 m b
21 06 12 f b
21 07 10 m b
21 08 10 m b
21 09 6 m b
21 10 1 f b

GLASSCOCK, Clemma

21 01 50 f b
21 02 44 f m
21 03 22 f b
21 04 21 f b
21 05 12 f b
21 06 4 f b
21 07 30 m b
21 08 27 m b
21 09 25 m b
21 10 12 m b
21 11 9 m b
21 12 2 m b
21 13 1 m b

JAMES, George

21 01 60 f m

GLADSON, Daniel
21 01 8 f b
BENEAR, Henry
21 01 16 m b
21 02 12 m b
21 03 20 f b
BENEAR, William H.
21 01 10 f b
SHAW, Alexander
21 01 10 m b
21 02 6 m m
WRIGHT, Harrison D.
21 01 50 m b
21 02 35 m b
21 03 35 f b
21 04 20 f b
21 05 10 f b
21 06 6 m b
21 07 4 f b
21 08 2 f b
21 09 9/12 m b
21 10 9/12 f b
MAGSBY, Daniel
21 01 70 m b
21 02 25 m b
McCORMICK, William
21 01 70 m b
21 02 21 m b
21 03 21 m b
21 04 25 f b
21 05 11 m b
21 06 10 m b
21 07 8 f b
21 08 7 m b
21 09 5 m b
21 10 4 m b
21 11 1 m b
21 12 1 f b
KNOLS, William
21 01 13 f b
GASKINS, Jno. H.
21 01 66 f b
21 02 61 m b
21 03 58 m b
21 04 55 m b
21 05 33 m b
21 06 17 m b
21 07 15 m b
21 08 39 f b
21 09 38 f b
21 10 23 f m
21 11 22 f b
21 12 10 f b
21 13 8 f b
21 14 3 f b
21 15 3 m b
21 16 3 m b
21 17 20 m b
21 18 4 m b
21 19 30 m b
BLACKWELL, William
21 01 40 m m
21 02 30 m b
21 03 28 m b
21 04 25 m m
21 05 27 m m
21 06 16 m b
21 07 25 f b
21 08 3 m m
22 09 2 f b
22 10 1 f b
22 11 16 f b
22 12 22 f b
JOURDON, M. H.
22 01 16 f b
DAWSON, Joseph
22 01 55 f b
22 02 22 m b
FOLEY, Elizabeth
22 01 45 f b
22 02 40 f b
22 03 27 m b
22 04 18 f b
22 05 16 m b
22 06 10 f b
22 07 10 f b
22 08 6 f b
22 09 6 f b
DIGGS, Sarah L.
22 01 85 f b
22 02 54 f b
22 03 26 f b
22 04 16 m b
22 05 10 f b
22 06 7 f b
22 07 3 f b

22 08 1 m b
22 09 3/12 m b

HUME, Thomas
22 01 12 m b

HUME, Jacob
22 01 50 f b
22 02 50 f b
22 03 40 f b
22 04 38 m b
22 05 42 m b
22 06 41 m b
22 07 27 m b
22 08 22 m b
22 09 21 m b
22 10 33 m b
22 11 30 m b
22 12 10 m b
22 13 8 m b
22 14 6 m b
22 15 16 f b
22 16 16 f b
22 17 6 f b
22 18 6 m b
22 19 7 f b
22 20 3 f b
22 21 9/12 f b

WHITESCARVER, George H.
22 01 46 f b
22 02 14 f b
22 03 20 m b
22 04 8 f b

TRIPLETT, Nathaniel
22 01 50 f b
22 02 21 m b
22 03 20 f b
22 04 17 m b
22 05 13 m b
22 06 12 m b
22 07 7 m b
22 08 4 m b
22 08 4 m b

HOLLAND, Ann
22 01 16 m b

PAYNE, William F.
22 01 50 m b
22 02 17 f b
22 03 13 f b
22 04 7 m b

PAYNE, James F.
22 01 25 f b
22 02 11 m b

DULIN, Catharine
22 01 25 f m
22 02 7 f m
22 03 6 f m
22 04 2 f m
22 05 1 m m

HURST, Capt. Mason
22 01 50 m b
22 02 37 f b
22 03 3 m b
22 04 50 f b

HURST, Thomas A.
22 01 10 m b
22 02 8 m b

RICE, William W.
22 01 24 f b
22 02 4 m b
22 03 45 f b

PAYNE, Thornton
22 01 55 f b
22 02 27 f m
22 03 21 f m
22 04 17 m m
23 05 17 f m
23 06 16 f b
23 07 13 m b
23 08 9 m b
23 09 6 f b
23 10 5 m b
23 11 3 m m
23 12 3 m b
23 13 2 m m
23 14 9/12 m m

FREEMAN, Thomas G.
23 01 50 f b
23 02 20 m m
23 03 15 f b

SMITH, Susan
23 01 60 f b

WITHERS, Thornton
23 01 75 f b
23 02 50 m b
23 03 30 m b
23 04 20 m b
23 05 15 m b

23 06 15 f m
23 07 10 f b
23 08 7 f b
23 09 5 f m
23 10 50 f b
23 11 60 m b
HOLTZCLAW, Charles W.
23 02 35 m b
23 02 21 m b
23 03 12 m b
CARVER, Baley
23 01 60 f b
23 02 50 m b
23 03 50 f b
23 04 28 m b
23 05 22 m b
23 06 24 f b
23 07 9 f b
23 08 6 m b
23 09 3 f b
23 10 14 f b
23 11 7 f b
ASHBY, Nimrod T.
23 01 70 f b
23 02 60 f b
23 03 42? f b
23 04 24 m b
23 05 62 m b
23 06 9 m b
23 07 7 f b
23 08 3 f b
23 09 3 m b
CHANCLER, Jno. H.
23 01 45 m b
23 02 30 m b
23 03 56 f b
23 04 30 f b
23 05 18 f b
23 06 16 m b
23 07 12 m b
23 08 8 f b
23 09 4 f b
23 10 5 m b
23 11 3 f b
PRIEST, Sarah
23 01 24 f b
23 02 9 m b
23 03 4 f m
23 04 4 m b
PAYNE, Frances
23 01 70 m b
23 02 22 m b
23 03 21 m b
23 04 21 m b
23 05 18 m b
23 06 30 f b
23 07 22 f b
23 08 20 f b
23 09 13 f b
23 10 5 m b
23 11 4 f b
23 12 4 m b
23 13 3 m b
23 14 1 m b
PAYNE, James
23 01 33 f b
23 02 13 f m
23 03 10 m b
23 04 7 f b
23 05 7 f b
23 06 3 f b
23 07 3 f b
24 08 6/12 m b
PAYNE, Maj'r. James
24 01 70 m b
24 02 60 f b
24 03 50 m b
24 04 30 m b
24 05 15 m b
24 06 14 f m
24 07 7 f b
24 08 7 f m
24 09 10 f m
24 10 4 m b
24 11 2 f b
24 12 4 m b
24 13 1 m b
PAYNE, Beraman
24 01 21 m b
24 02 20 m b
24 03 10 m b
24 04 19 f b
24 05 16 f b
24 06 4/12 m b
24 07 7 m b
24 08 6 f m

24 09 4 m b
24 10 2 m b

JOHNSON, Thomas
24 01 24 f b
24 02 3 f b
24 03 10/12 f b

LITTLE, Left? Jno. H.
24 01 45 f b
24 02 18 f b
24 03 33 m m
24 04 19 m b
24 05 15 m b

KIRTS, Frances
24 01 55 m b
24 02 40 f m
24 03 4 f b

FOLEY, Andrew C.
24 01 50 f b
24 02 35 m b
24 03 17 m b

PAYNE, William W.
24 01 15 f b
24 02 11 f b

BARBEE, Joseph A.
24 01 40 f b
24 02 17 m b
24 03 13 f b

EDWARDS, William
24 01 223 f b

PAYNE, James W.
24 01 18 f b

PARSONS, Stephen
24 01 17 f b
24 02 10 m b

McDANIEL, Balis
24 01 16 m m

HERROLL, Jno.
24 01 60 f b

STROTHER, Edgman
24 01 50 m b
24 02 20 f b
24 03 16 f b
24 04 13 f b
24 05 8 m b
24 06 7 f b
24 07 3 m b
24 08 3 m b
24 09 1 m b

UTTERBACK, Elias
24 01 30 f b
24 02 17 m b
24 03 9 m m
24 04 5 f m
24 05 3 f m
24 06 3 m m

DICKSON, Henry
24 01 85 m b
24 02 84 f b

JOHNSON, Smith
24 01 65 f b
24 02 40 f b
24 03 5 m b
24 04 2 f b

Parish slaves
24 01 80 f b
24 02 80 f b
24 03 79 f b
24 04 95 f b

BARBER, Enoch
24 01 32 f b
24 02 8 f m
24 03 5 m b
24 04 2 m b
24 05 25 m b

LALLER, Willace
24 01 9 f b

BURK, Jno. T.
24 01 16 m m
24 02 12 m m

McQUIN, George
24 01 65 f b

Riley, Wesly
24 01 14 m b
24 02 ? ? m

PUTMAN, Levi J.
25 01 40 m m
25 02 25 f m
25 03 10 f b
25 04 7 f m
25 05 5 m m
25 06 6/12 f m

BALL, Joseph
25 01 46 f b
25 02 20 m b
25 03 18 m m
25 04 6 f m

WINES, James
25 01 16 f b
25 02 2 m m
LAKE, Richard E.
25 01 40 m b
25 02 26 m b
25 03 22 m b
25 04 50 m b
25 05 25 f b
25 06 18 f b
25 07 10 m b
25 08 6 f b
25 09 4 m b
25 10 2 f b
25 11 2 f b
25 12 6/12 m b
JACKSON, Jno. F.
25 01 33 f b
25 02 15 m b
25 03 9 f b
25 04 4 m b
25 05 1 f b
HOPE, James W.
25 01 60 m b
25 02 55 m b
25 03 50 m b
25 04 50 m b
25 05 22 m b
25 06 17 m b
25 07 11 m b
25 08 11 m b
25 09 26 f b
25 10 22 f b
25 11 1 f b
25 12 8/12 f b
25 13 6 f b
MADDOX, James
25 01 17 f b
25 02 13 f b
25 03 40 m b
BARKER, Jno.
25 01 65 m b
25 02 60 f b
25 03 54 f b
25 04 40 m b
25 05 28 m b
25 06 26 m b
25 07 26 m b
25 08 26 f b
25 09 26 f b
25 10 17 m b
25 11 14 f b
25 12 23 m b
25 13 11 m b
25 14 8 m b
25 15 5 m b
25 16 5 m b
25 17 5 m b
25 18 22 f b
25 19 9/12 m b
25 20 9/12 f b
GLASSCOCK, Samuel
25 01 57 m b
25 02 55 m b
25 03 24 m b
25 04 23 m b
25 05 45 f b
25 06 20 f b
25 07 14 m b
LAKE, William
25 01 30 f b
25 02 26 m b
25 03 24 m b
25 04 17 m b
25 05 16 m b
25 06 13 m b
25 07 10 m b
25 08 10 f b
25 09 1 f b
WRIGHT, Doct. W. B.
25 01 57 f b
25 02 53 m b
25 03 21 m b
26 04 30 m b
26 05 16 m b
26 06 21 f b
26 07 18 f b
26 08 3 m b
26 09 2 m b
26 10 7/12 m b
26 11 9/12 m b
NEWMAN, Doct. Jno. W.
26 01 45 m b
26 02 45 m b
26 03 22 f b
26 04 4 f b

26 05 2 m b
STROTHER, Jno.
26 01 75 m b
26 02 50 f b
26 03 53 m b
26 04 40 m m
26 05 40 m b
26 06 33 m m
26 07 30 m b
26 08 27 f b
26 09 25 m b
26 10 27 f b
26 11 14 m b
26 12 14 f b
26 13 12 m b
26 14 10 m b
26 15 10 f b
26 16 8 f b
26 17 8 f b
26 18 6 f b
26 19 6 f b
26 20 4 m b
26 21 5 f b
26 22 4 m b
26 23 2 m b
26 24 1 f b
26 25 6/12 m b
STEPHENS, David
26 01 40 f b
26 02 18 m b
26 03 8 m b
26 04 8/12 f b
THOMPSON, James S.
26 01 68 m b
26 02 36 m b
26 03 25 f b
26 04 13 f b
26 05 4 f b
CARTER, Josiah
26 01 55 m m
26 02 48 f b
26 03 34 f b
26 04 15 f b
26 05 17 m b
26 06 10 m m
26 07 8 f m
26 08 6 f b
26 09 8/12 f b
26 10 22 m b
HORNER, Richard B.
26 01 65 f b
26 02 45 f b
26 03 40 m b
26 04 42 m b
26 05 16 m b
26 06 17 f b
26 07 12 f b
26 08 8 m b
26 09 10 f b
26 10 5 f b
26 11 30 f b
26 12 4 f b
26 13 2 m b
26 14 9/12 f b
CARVER, James
26 01 60 m b
26 02 46 m b
26 03 24 m b
26 04 9 m b
26 05 40 f b
26 06 18 f b
26 07 18 f b
26 08 8 f b
26 09 1 f b
26 10 5/12 f b
26 11 3/12 m b
EALRY [EARLY], Jno.
26 01 64 f b
26 02 ? f ?
SMITH, P. H.
26 01 35 f b
26 02 35 f b
26 03 19 m b
26 04 11 m b
26 05 9 f b
26 06 7 f b
26 07 6 m b
26 08 2 f b
26 09 1 m b
26 10 40 f b
26 11 9 m b
BRADLEY, Presly G.
26 01 30 m b
26 02 12 f b
26 03 4 f b
26 04 8 f b

COCHRAN, Hezekiah
26 01 100 f b
26 02 60 f b
26 03 23 f b
26 04 50 f b
26 05 19 f b
26 06 12 f b
26 07 20 m b
26 08 18 m b
26 09 17 m b
26 10 4 m b
26 11 3 m b
26 12 6 m b
26 13 3 f b
26 14 1 f b
26 15 8/12 f b
STROTHER, Susan
26 01 42 f b
26 02 42 m b
26 03 30 m b
26 04 23 f b
26 05 22 f b
26 06 8 m b
26 07 6 m b
26 08 5 m b
26 09 4 f b
26 10 4 m b
26 11 4 m b
FLETCHER, Jno. W.
26 01 42 m b
McCLANAHAN, Jno.
26 01 10 f m
26 02 5 f b
FLETCHER, Margarett E.
26 01 10 m b
WALDEN, Col. Jno.
26 01 70 m b
26 02 60 m m
26 03 34 m m
26 04 21 m m
26 05 18 m b
26 06 18 m b
26 07 14 m b
26 08 8 m b
26 09 5 m m
26 10 3 m m
26 11 50 f b
26 12 36 f b
26 13 22 f m
26 14 23 f b
26 15 21 f b
GASKINS, Alfred
26 01 52 m b
26 02 38 m b
26 03 22 m b
26 04 16 m b
26 05 9 m b
26 06 4 m b
26 07 40 f b
26 08 24 f b
26 09 21 f b
26 10 20 f b
26 11 16 f b
26 12 12 f b
26 13 10 f b
26 14 9 f b
26 15 1 f b
26 16 6/12 m b
26 17 3 m b
26 18 1 m b
RANDLE, Horace C.
26 01 70 f b
JEFFERS [JEFFRIES], Joseph
26 01 55 f b
26 02 40 m b
26 03 25 m b
26 04 27 f b
26 05 25 f b
27 06 11 f b
27 07 9 m b
27 08 4 m b
BLACKWELL, Joseph
27 01 30 m b
27 02 29 m b
27 03 16 m b
27 04 14 m b
27 05 5 m b
27 06 4 m b
27 07 8/12 m b
27 08 45 f b
27 09 23 f b
27 10 13 f b
27 11 12 f m
27 12 2 f b
BALL, Fenton
27 01 7 f m

FLETCHER, Alexander D.
27 01 12 f b
GANES, Lewis H.
27 01 45 m b
27 02 43 m b
27 03 28 m b
27 04 29 m b
27 05 12 m b
27 06 4 m b
27 07 32 f b
27 08 3 f b
MOFFETT, Jno. A.
27 01 20 f b
27 02 6 f b
27 03 2 f b
NELSON, Fanny
27 01 60 f b
27 02 60 m b
27 03 50 m b
27 04 40 m b
27 05 17 m b
27 06 35 f b
27 07 6 m b
27 08 5 f b
27 09 2 f b
DIGGS, Edward
27 01 60 m b
27 02 35 f b
27 03 25 f b
27 04 17 f b
27 05 14 m b
27 06 12 f b
27 07 10 f b
27 08 8 f b
27 09 4 f b
27 10 1 f b
DIGGS, Thomas E.
27 01 60 m b
27 02 47 m b
27 03 28 f b
27 04 27 f b
27 05 24 f b
27 06 20 f b
27 07 8 f b
27 08 6 f b
27 09 3 f b
27 10 10/12 m b
MOOR, George
27 01 24 f b
27 02 19 m b
27 03 19 m b
27 04 4 f b
27 05 2 f b
KEITH, Mary L.
27 01 65 m b
27 02 40 f b
27 03 30 f b
27 04 35 m b
27 05 22 m b
27 06 16 m b
27 07 14 f b
27 08 9 m b
27 09 9 f b
CURNS [KERNS], Marshall
27 01 80 f b
McCOY, Walter B.
27 01 58 f b
27 02 53 f b
27 03 53 m b
27 04 10 f b
27 05 6 m m
HALL, Thomas
27 01 26 f m
27 02 3 m m
27 03 2 m m
PAYNE, William W.
27 01 37 f b
27 02 16 f b
27 03 10 m b
27 04 ? f b
28 05 4 f b
28 06 2 m b
28 07 37 m b
28 08 26 m b
PAYNE, A. M.
28 01 70 f b
28 02 60 m b
28 03 56 m b
28 04 55 m b
28 05 44 m b
28 06 37 m b
28 07 35 m b
28 08 45 m b
28 09 33 m b
28 10 25 m b
28 11 16 m b

28 12 10 m b
28 13 5 m b
28 14 3 m b
28 15 35 f b
28 16 33 f b
28 17 27 f b
28 18 23 f b
28 19 22 f b
28 20 40 f b
28 21 20 f b
28 22 17 f b
28 23 13 f b
28 24 6 f b
28 25 5 f b
28 26 1 f b
28 27 5 f b
28 28 3 f b
28 29 1 f b
28 30 1 f b
28 31 1 m b

JEFFERS [JEFFRIES], Enoch

28 01 45 f b
28 02 34 f b
28 03 7 f b
28 04 20 f b
28 05 19 f b
28 06 16 f b
28 07 71? m b
28 08 5 m b
28 09 5 m b
28 10 4 f b
28 11 3 m b
28 12 1 f b
28 13 1 f b

BALEY, Nancy

28 01 55 f b
28 02 55 m b
28 03 26 f b
28 04 18 m b
28 05 8 f b
28 06 6 m b
28 07 5 f b
28 08 4 f b
28 09 1 m b

SCOTT, Mrs. Judy

28 01 65 f b
28 02 50 f b
28 03 47 f m
28 04 45 f m
28 05 44 f b
28 06 40 f b
28 07 40 f b
28 08 24 f b
28 09 24 f b
28 10 23 f m
28 11 23 f b
28 12 24 f b
28 13 25 f b
28 14 24 f b
28 15 17 f b
28 16 16 f b
28 17 27 f b
28 18 25 f b
28 19 24 f b
28 20 12 f m
28 21 10 f m
28 22 9 f m
28 23 7 f b
28 24 5 m b
28 25 6 m b
28 26 5 m b
28 27 4 m b
29 28 3 m b
29 29 2 m b
29 30 1 m b
29 31 7 m b
29 32 55 m b
29 33 30 m b
29 34 30 m b
29 35 26 m b
29 36 25 m b
29 37 20 m b
29 38 18 m b
29 39 17 m b
29 40 16 m b
29 41 14 m b
29 42 12 m b
29 43 12 m b
29 44 10 m b
29 45 10 m b
29 46 9 m b
29 47 9 m b
29 48 17 m b
29 49 40 m b
29 50 35 m b
29 51 25 m b

29 52 30 m b
29 53 8 m b
29 54 6 f b
29 55 5 f b
29 56 3 f b

PAYNE, Marshall
29 01 45 f b

FISHER, Frank
29 01 25 m b
29 02 18 f b
29 03 2 f b

FISHER, Jno.
29 01 54 m b
29 02 30 m b
29 03 30 m b
29 04 30 f b
29 05 18 f b
29 06 6 f b
29 07 4 f b
29 08 6/12 f b

LIONS, Jno.
29 01 14 f b

HELM, Erasmus
29 01 56 m b
29 02 30 m b
29 03 25 m b
29 04 37 f b
29 05 15 f b

PIGGOTT, Capt. George
29 01 52 m b
29 02 30 f b
29 03 30 m b
29 04 29 m b
29 05 28 m b
29 06 20 f b
29 07 18 f m
29 08 15 m b
29 09 15 f b
29 10 10 f b
29 11 12 f b
29 12 6 m b
29 13 3 f b
29 14 7/12 m b
29 15 7/12 f b
29 16 25 f b
29 17 20 f b
29 18 15 f b

HITT, Rhuben
29 01 20 f b
29 02 20 m b
29 03 5 f m
29 04 9/12 f b
29 05 45 f b

PAYNE, Daniel
29 01 70 f b
29 02 70 f b
29 03 33 f b
29 04 28 f b
29 05 43 f b
29 06 56 m b
29 07 50 m b
29 08 50 m b
29 09 23 m b
29 10 20 m b
29 11 9 m b
29 12 8 m m
29 13 ? m b
29 14 ? ? ?
30 15 2 m m

HART, Robt.
30 01 60 m b
30 02 55 m b
30 03 40 m b
30 04 28 m b
30 05 23 m b
30 06 19 m b
30 07 15 m b
30 08 7 m b
30 09 3 m b
30 10 40 f b
30 11 33 f b
30 12 24 f b
30 13 19 f b
30 14 14 f b
30 15 10 f b
30 16 10 f b
30 17 10 f b
30 18 3 f b
30 19 1 f b
30 20 25 f b
30 21 9 f b
30 22 7 f b
30 23 5 m b
30 24 2 f b

HART, Arthur
30 01 50 m b

30 02 50 f b
30 03 25 f b
30 04 10 f b
HART, Jno.
30 01 22 f b
30 02 20 f m
30 03 20 m b
30 04 12 f b
30 05 1 m b
CARVER, William
30 01 76 f b
30 02 40 m b
30 03 27 m b
30 04 12 m b
30 05 1 f b
PORTER,Samuel
30 01 30 m b
PORTER, Jno.
30 01 60 f b
30 02 45 f b
30 03 45 m b
30 04 35 m b
30 05 35 m b
30 06 28 m b
30 07 25 f b
30 08 20 f b
30 09 18 m b
30 10 13 m b
30 11 13 m b
30 12 11 m b
30 13 11 f b
30 14 11 f b
30 15 10 f b
30 16 9 f b
30 17 7 f b
30 18 6 f b
30 19 4 m b
30 20 2 f m
30 21 15 f b
30 22 9/12 f b
30 23 4 m b
30 24 4 m b
30 25 9/12 m b
THOMPSON, Ann
30 01 64 f b
BLYHT, Doct. Saml.
30 01 50 m b
30 02 35 m b
30 03 34 f b
30 04 22 m b
30 05 22 m b
30 06 20 f b
30 07 17 f b
30 08 13 m b
30 09 8 f b
30 10 6 m b
30 11 4 f b
30 12 1 f b
HOLTSCLAW, Francis
30 01 50 m b
30 02 35 f b
30 03 19 f b
30 04 7 f b
31 05 2 f b
31 06 1 m b
CARTER, William W.
31 01 60 f b
31 02 24 f m
31 03 24 m m
31 04 22 m b
31 05 16 f m
31 06 15 m m
31 07 11 f b
31 08 3 f b
31 09 1 m b
NELSON, Thomas
31 01 40 f b
31 02 13 m b
31 03 3 m m
31 04 1 f b
BEAL, William
31 01 25 m b
31 02 18 m b
31 03 45 f b
31 04 25 f m
31 05 16 f m
31 06 14 m m
31 07 12 f m
31 08 10 f m
31 09 8 m m
31 10 6 f m
31 11 4 m m
31 12 1 f m
31 13 1 f b
31 14 20 m b *

* deaf

BROOK, Marton P.

31	01	75	m	b
31	02	35	m	b
31	03	30	m	b
31	04	28	m	b
31	05	24	f	b
31	06	27	f	b
31	07	23	m	b
31	08	14	f	b
31	09	12	m	b
31	10	9	m	b
31	11	8	m	b
31	12	4	m	b
31	13	10	f	b
31	14	4	f	b
31	15	2	f	b
31	16	5	m	b
31	17	9/12	m	b

KEITH, Isham

31	01	60	m	b
31	02	60	f	b
31	03	55	m	b
31	04	50	m	b
31	05	50	f	b
31	06	22	f	b
31	07	21	f	b
31	08	24	f	b
31	09	30	m	b
31	10	27	m	b
31	11	21	m	b
31	12	25	m	b
31	13	20	m	b
31	14	15	m	b
31	15	4	f	b
31	16	3	f	b
31	17	3	f	b
31	18	2	m	b
31	19	1	f	b

McNISH, William

31	01	75	f	b
31	02	35	m	b
31	03	50	m	b
31	04	53	m	b
31	05	45	m	b
31	06	40	m	b
31	07	50	m	b
31	08	43	m	m
31	09	20	m	b
31	10	23	m	b
31	11	25	m	m
31	12	25	m	b
31	13	23	m	m
31	14	30	m	b
31	15	19	m	b
31	16	15	m	m
31	17	16	m	b
31	18	15	m	b
31	19	40?	m	m
32	20	19	f	b
32	21	16	m	b
32	22	50	f	b
32	23	45	m	m

GREEN, Eleanor

32	01	19	f	b
32	02	10	f	b
32	03	1	m	m

FLIN, Samuel

32	01	18	f	b

PETERS, James

32	01	21	f	b
32	02	16	m	b
32	03	14	f	b
32	04	10	f	b
32	05	3	m	b

ALLEN, Capt. Fielding

32	01	30	m	m
32	02	26	f	m
32	03	26	f	b
32	04	14	f	m
32	05	7	f	m
32	06	5	m	m
32	07	2	f	b
32	08	2	f	m
32	09	12	m	b
32	10	9	m	m

LLOYD, James

32	01	10	f	b

McCOY, William

32	01	85	f	b
32	02	45	m	b
32	03	28	m	b
32	04	25	f	b
32	05	20	f	b
32	06	15	m	m
32	07	12	f	b
32	08	10	f	b

32 09 8 f b
32 10 5 m b
32 11 3 f b
32 12 2 f b

CARTER, George
32 01 90 f b
32 02 70 f b
32 03 45 f b
32 04 32 f b
32 05 18 m b
32 06 10 m b
32 07 7 f b
32 08 5 m b
32 09 4 f b
32 10 11 m m
32 11 22 m b

WITHERS, Majr. Jessa H.
32 01 80 f b
32 02 50 m b
32 03 45 f b
32 04 40 f b
32 05 19 m b
32 06 18 m b
32 07 14 m b
32 08 11 m b
32 09 9 f b
32 10 8 f b
32 11 6 f b
32 12 14 f b

HUDNAL, William
32 01 70 f b
32 02 60 m b
32 03 40 m b
32 04 25 m b
32 05 20 f b
32 06 19 f b *
* idiotic
32 07 10 m b
32 08 8 m b
32 09 7 m b
32 10 1 m b

HUDNAL, Albert
32 01 23 f m
32 02 3 f m
32 03 1 f m
32 04 57 m b

ROSE, Mary S. H.
32 01 58 m b
32 02 45 m b
32 03 40 m b
32 04 55 m b
32 05 25 m b
32 06 14 m b
32 07 70 f b
32 08 65 f b
32 09 60 f b
32 10 40 f b
32 11 25 f b
32 12 22 f b
32 13 23? f b
33 14 20 f b
33 15 7 f b

ROSE, William A.
33 01 75 m b
33 02 75 f b
33 03 12 m b
33 04 9 m b
33 05 40 f b
33 06 5 f b
33 07 2 f b
33 08 20 f b
33 09 1 f b
33 10 16 m b

NELSON, George
33 01 58 f b
33 02 40 f b
33 03 30 f m
33 04 25 f m
33 05 10 f m
33 06 12 f m
33 07 10 f m
33 08 6 f m
33 09 5 f b
33 10 6 f m
33 11 5 m b
33 12 30 m b
33 13 25 m b
33 14 25 m b
33 15 24 m m
33 16 16 f b

RUSSEL, Samuel
33 01 50 m b
33 02 50 m m
33 03 45 m b
33 04 20 m b
33 05 16 m m

33	06	50	f	b
33	07	10	f	m
33	08	65	f	b

BISPHAM, William N.

33	01	52	f	b
33	02	29	f	b
33	03	28	m	b
33	04	16	m	b
33	05	12	m	b
33	06	11	f	b
33	07	8	m	b
33	08	6	f	b
33	09	5	m	b
33	10	2	f	b
33	11	2	m	b

INGLISH, Zebaniah R.

33	01	40	f	m
33	02	23	f	m
33	03	20	f	b
33	04	18	m	b
33	05	15	f	m
33	06	10	m	b
33	07	7	m	b
33	08	5	m	b
33	09	3	f	b
33	10	5	f	m

BRADFORD, Catharine

33	01	50	m	b
33	02	45	m	b
33	03	44	m	b
33	04	43	m	b
33	05	24	m	b
33	06	23	m	b
33	07	22	m	b
33	08	18	m	b
33	09	12	m	b
33	10	10	m	b
33	11	6	m	b
33	12	5	m	b
33	13	3	m	b
33	14	1	m	b
33	15	1	m	b
33	16	50	f	b
33	17	40	f	b
33	18	35	f	b
33	19	21	f	b
33	20	16	f	b
33	21	14	f	b
33	22	12	f	b
33	23	9	f	b
33	24	2	f	b
33	25	4	f	b

LOVEL, Alice T.

33	01	80	m	b
33	02	47?	m	b
34	03	17	m	b
34	04	16	m	b
34	05	14	m	b
34	06	10	m	b
34	07	49	f	b
34	08	25	f	b
34	09	10	f	b
34	10	8	f	b
34	11	6	f	b
34	12	4	f	b

ASHTON, Elizabeth

34	01	45	m	b
34	02	34	f	b
34	03	23	f	b
34	04	5	m	b
34	05	4	m	b
34	06	2	f	b
34	07	6/12	m	b

LEE, Jno. A.

34	01	90	m	b
34	02	73	m	b
34	03	50	m	b
34	04	50	f	b
34	05	43	f	b
34	06	30	f	m
34	07	26	f	b
34	08	22	m	b
34	09	20	f	m
34	10	16	m	b
34	11	14	m	b
34	12	12	m	b
34	13	10	f	b
34	14	11	f	b
34	15	9	f	b
34	16	7	m	b
34	17	7	f	b
34	18	7	m	b
34	19	4	m	b
34	20	4	m	b
34	21	4	f	b
34	22	4	m	b

34 23 2 f b
34 24 2 f b
34 25 1 m m
34 26 22 m b
RIEN, Lewis A.
34 01 84 f b
34 02 12 f b
OLENGER, Osker
34 01 40 m b
34 02 14 m b
34 03 40 f b
CRUMP, Nathaniel N.
34 01 55 f b
34 02 35 m b
34 03 38 f b
34 04 23 f b
34 05 12 f b
34 06 11 m b
34 07 7 f b
34 08 4 f b
34 09 4 f b
34 10 2 m b
34 11 1 m b
34 12 4 m b
ROUT, Alphonso
34 01 35 f b
34 02 25 f b
34 03 10 m m
34 04 7 f m
34 05 3 m m
HARRIS, Elizabeth
34 01 10 m b
WITHERS, Jno. W.
34 01 45 f b
UTZ, Briget?
34 01 45 f b
34 02 8 m b
HACKLY, George B.
34 01 12 f b
NORMAN, Peyton
34 01 90 m b
34 02 90 f b
34 03 49 m b
34 04 48 m b
34 05 40 f b
34 06 21 m b
34 07 14 f b
34 08 12 m b
34 09 7 f b
34 10 5 f b
34 11 2 m b
FANT, Jno. M.
34 01 70 m b
34 02 70 m b
34 03 4 m b
35 04 25 m b
35 05 20 m b
35 06 19 m b
35 07 17 m b
35 08 15 m b
35 09 12 m b
35 10 12 m b
35 11 11 m b
35 12 12 m b
35 13 9 m b
35 14 9 m b
35 15 7 m b
35 16 50 f b
35 17 40 f b
35 18 35 f b
35 19 30 f b
35 20 35 f b
35 21 37 f b
35 22 18 f b
35 23 16 f b
35 24 15 f b
35 25 10 f b
35 26 9 f b
35 27 4 f b
35 28 3 f b
35 29 2 f b
35 30 2 f b
35 31 3 f b
35 32 1 f b
FREEMAN, Stephen
35 01 90 f b
35 02 38 f b
35 03 10 f b
35 04 4 f b
35 05 58 m b
35 06 52 m b
35 07 29 m b
35 08 6 m b
FREEMAN, James
35 01 60 f b
35 02 50 m b

35 03 25 m b
35 04 16 f b
35 05 13 m b

JAMES, Capt. David

35 01 75 m b
35 02 21 m b
35 03 18 m b
35 04 35 f b
35 05 32 f b
35 06 13 f b
35 07 11 f m
35 08 40 f m
35 09 8 f m
35 10 6 f m
35 11 35 m b

DULANY, Ann

35 01 75 m b
35 02 65 m b
35 03 50 m b
35 04 45 m b
35 05 50 m b
35 06 45 m b
35 07 40 m b
35 08 40 m b
35 09 25 m b
35 10 23 m b
35 11 25 m b
35 12 20 m b
35 13 19 m b
35 14 18 m b
35 15 17 m m
35 16 15 m b
35 17 14 m b
35 18 14 m b
35 19 12 m b
35 20 12 m b
35 21 10 m b
35 22 11 m b
35 23 10 m m
35 24 10 m b
35 25 7 m b
35 26 5 m m
35 27 7 m m
35 28 8 m b
35 29 5 m b
35 30 2 m b
35 31 1? m b
36 32 40 m b
36 33 3 m b
36 34 7 m b
36 35 3 m b
36 36 5 m b
36 37 1 m b
36 38 2 m b
36 39 2 m b
36 40 50 f b
36 41 8 f b
36 42 45 f b
36 43 23 f b
36 44 20 f b
36 45 7 f b
36 46 6 f b
36 47 5 f b
36 48 4 f b
36 49 2 f b
36 50 50 f b
36 51 20 f b
36 52 8 f b
36 53 9 f b
36 54 6 f b
36 55 4 f b
36 56 2 f b
36 57 60 f b
36 58 4 f b
36 59 2 f b
36 60 2 f b
36 61 23 f b
36 62 6 f b
36 63 4 f b
36 64 3 f b
36 65 2 f b
36 66 1 f b
36 67 55 f b
36 68 26 f b
36 69 20 f b
36 70 18 f b
36 71 21 f b
36 72 20 f b
36 73 3 f b
36 74 36 f b
36 75 21 f b
36 76 3 f b
36 77 2 f b
36 78 1 f b
36 79 1 f b
36 80 58 f b

36 81 14 f b
36 82 14 f b
36 83 28 f b
36 84 20 f b
36 85 8 f b
36 86 4 f b
36 87 1 f b
36 88 1 f b
36 89 30 f b
36 90 16 f b
36 91 10 f b
36 92 5 f b
36 93 3 f b
36 94 1 f b
36 95 1 f b
36 96 45 f b
36 97 20 f b
36 98 10 f m
36 99 3 f b
36 100 4 f b
36 101 36 f m
36 102 2 f b
36 103 2 f b

FOX, Jno.

36 01 70 m m
36 02 65 m b
36 03 65 m b
36 04 50 m m
36 05 39 m m
36 06 36 m b
36 07 26 m b
36 08 25 m b
36 09 24 m b
36 10 18 m b
36 11 14 m b
36 12 11 m b
36 13 12 m b
37 14 6 m b
37 15 5 m b
37 16 5 m b
37 17 7 m b
37 18 4 m m
37 19 5 m m
37 20 5 m m
37 21 5 m m
37 22 5 m m
37 23 3 m b
37 24 3 m b
37 25 3 m b
37 26 3 m b
37 27 6 m m
37 28 7 m b
37 29 6 m b
37 30 5 m b
37 31 6/12 f m
37 32 6 f m
37 33 7 f m
37 34 7 f b
37 35 7 f m
37 36 5 f b
37 37 4 f b
37 38 3 f b
37 39 1 f b
37 40 6/12 f b
37 41 3 f b
37 42 7/12 f b
37 43 70 ff b
37 44 55 f b
37 45 45 f b
37 46 40 f b
37 47 30 f b
37 48 25 f b
37 49 20 f b
37 50 16 f b
37 51 20 f b
37 52 25 f b

DAY, Paul W.

37 01 55 m b
37 02 45 f b
37 03 35 f b
37 04 22 m b
37 05 20 m b
37 06 14 f b
37 07 11 m b

BUTLER, Carter

37 01 13 f m
37 02 50 m m
37 03 25 f m
37 04 8 f m
37 05 6 m m
37 06 1 m m

REID, Coalman

37 01 65 f b
37 02 34 f b
37 03 22 m b
37 04 18 m b

37 05 7 f b
37 06 4 m b
37 07 2 m b

ASHTON, Thomas S.
37 01 40 f b
37 02 11 f b

NEWHOUSE, Silas
37 01 50 f b
37 02 70 m b
37 03 9 f b

OLENGER, Elizabeth
37 01 35 f b
37 02 24 m b
37 03 22 m b
37 04 7 m b
37 05 5 m b
37 06 40 m b

HIRD, William
37 01 20 f m
37 02 6/12 m m

WILLS, Robt.
37 01 12 f b

DUFF, Capt. George
37 01 9 m b

GROVES, James O.
37 01 8 f b

DODD, Sanford
37 01 65 m b
37 02 87 f b

DODD, Jno.
37 01 75 m b
37 02 50 f b
37 03 34 m b
37 04 22 m b
37 05 19 f b
37 06 9 f b
37 07 9 m b

WILLS, Robt.
38 01 23 m b
38 02 22 m b
38 03 12 f b

RIEN, Christopher
38 01 30 f m
38 02 11 f m
38 03 9 f m
38 04 7 f m
38 05 5 f m
38 06 5/12 f m

WILLIAMS, Bazell
38 01 60 f b

BOWEN, Stephen
38 01 40 f b
38 02 30 m b
38 03 13 m b
38 04 10 m b
38 05 25 m b
38 06 2 m b

GROVES, Samuel F.
38 01 20 f b
38 02 1 m b

RIEN, Wesly
38 01 12 m b

SOTHARD, Margarett
38 01 26 f m
38 02 21 m m
38 03 22 m b
38 04 15 m b
38 05 10 f m
38 06 8 m b
38 07 6 m b
38 08 5 m b
38 09 4 f b
38 10 3 f b
38 11 18 f b

RECTOR, Thompson
38 01 100 f b
38 02 40 f b
38 03 9 m b
38 04 9/12 m b

CANER, Jno.
38 01 15 f b

FRANKLIN, William E.
38 01 45 m b
38 02 35 m b
38 03 40 f b
38 04 30 f b
38 05 25 f b
38 06 18 f b
38 07 18 f b
38 07 12 m b
38 08 10 m b
38 09 10 m b
38 10 9 f b
38 11 7 f b
38 12 6 f b
38 13 6 f b

38	14	5	m	b
38	15	4	m	b
38	16	4	m	b
38	17	2	f	b
38	18	2	f	b
38	19	80	f	b

DOWNMAN, Jno. B.

38	01	90	f	b
38	02	58	f	b
38	03	40	f	b
38	04	36	f	b
38	05	36	f	b
38	06	32	f	b
38	07	30	f	b
38	08	27	f	b
38	09	18	f	b
38	10	18	f	b
38	11	23	f	b
38	12	14	f	b
38	13	6	f	b
38	14	6	f	b
38	15	6	f	b
38	16	56	m	b
38	17	35	m	b
38	18	35	m	b
38	19	32	m	b
38	20	34	m	b
38	21	29	m	b
38	22	29	m	b
38	23	25	m	b
38	24	21	m	b
38	25	21	m	b
38	26	13	m	b
38	27	12	m	b
38	28	12	m	b
38	29	14	m	b
39	30	10	m	b
39	31	10	m	b
39	32	9	m	b
39	33	8	m	b
39	34	8	m	b
39	35	7	m	b
39	36	5	m	b
39	37	4	m	b
39	38	3	m	b
39	39	4	m	b
39	40	2	m	b
39	41	1	m	b
39	42	6/12	m	b

THORN, Jno. C.

39	01	50	m	b
39	02	45	m	b
39	03	11	m	b
39	04	20	m	b
39	05	45	f	b
39	06	20	f	m
39	07	16	f	b

BOWEN, William A.

39	01	55	f	b
39	02	24	f	b
39	03	25	f	m
39	04	21	f	m
39	05	26	f	b
39	06	5	f	m
39	07	2	f	m
39	08	3	f	b
39	09	2	f	b
39	10	45	m	b
39	11	60	m	b
39	12	30	m	b
39	13	26	m	b
39	14	25	m	b
39	15	24	m	b
39	16	24	m	b
39	17	21	m	b
39	18	65	m	b
39	19	27	m	b
39	20	26	m	b
39	21	9	m	b
39	22	10	m	b
39	23	18	f	m

MOOR, Catharine R.

39	01	40	f	b
39	02	43	f	b
39	03	21	f	b
39	04	12	f	b
39	05	5	f	m
39	06	3	f	b
39	07	55	m	b
39	08	14	m	b
39	09	7	m	b

HAMILTON, Doct. Hugh

39	01	45	m	b
39	02	40	m	b
39	03	36	m	m
39	04	32	m	b

39 05 29 m b
39 06 24 m b
39 07 20 m b
39 08 14 m b
39 09 7 m b
39 10 7 m b
39 11 2 m b
39 12 33 f b
39 13 32 f b
39 14 28 f b
39 15 27 f b
39 16 26 f b
39 17 15 f b
39 18 9 f b
39 19 14 f b
39 20 9 f b
39 21 4 f b
39 22 13 f b
39 23 9 f b
39 24 5 f b
39 25 2 f b
39 26 7 f b
39 27 9 f b
39 28 12 f b

KNOX, Jno. S.

39 01 70 m m
39 02 55 m m
39 03 30 m b
39 04 40 m? b
40 05 30 m b
40 06 18 m b
40 07 15 m b
40 08 11 m b
40 09 10 m b
40 10 9 m b
40 11 9 m b
40 12 55 f b
40 13 28 f b
40 14 24 f b
40 15 20 f b
40 16 6 f b
40 17 4 f b
40 18 6/12 f b
40 19 3 f b
40 20 45 f b

COALMAN, Wilson

40 01 25 f b

BURIS, Samuel

40 01 50 f b
40 02 30 m b
40 03 25 m b
40 04 18 m b
40 05 19 m b
40 06 18 f b
40 07 25 f b
40 08 8 f m
40 09 5 m b
40 10 3 m b
40 11 3 f b
40 12 1 f b

KELLY, Granville

40 01 50 m b
40 02 45 m b
40 03 39 f b
40 04 40 f b
40 05 20 m m
40 06 17 f b
40 07 18 f m
40 08 13 m b
40 09 12 m b
40 10 10 f b
40 11 8 m b
40 12 7 m b
40 13 4 m b
40 14 4 m b
40 15 3 f b
40 16 1 f b
40 17 2 f b

CLOPTON, Doct. Nathaniel V.

40 01 80 f b
40 02 75 f b
40 03 70 f b
40 04 62 f b
40 05 60 m b
40 06 43 m b
40 07 41 m m
40 08 33 m b
40 09 45 m b
40 10 30 m b
40 11 25 m b
40 12 20 m m
40 13 18 m b
40 14 17 m b
40 15 16 m b
40 16 12 m m
40 17 16 m b

40 18 10 m b
40 19 10 m b
40 20 8 m b
40 21 6 m b
40 22 3 m m
40 23 42 f b
40 24 39 f m *
* only one leg
40 25 36 f b
40 26 34 f b
40 27 19 f b
40 28 9 f m
40 29 8 f b
40 30 7 f m
40 31 4 f m
40 32 4 f b
40 33 6/12 m b
40 34 5 f b

GREEN, Robt.
40 01 60 f b
40 02 40 f b
40 03 18 m b
40 04 15 f b
41 05 15 f b
41 06 12 m b
41 07 10 m b
41 08 10 m b
41 09 4 m b
41 10 2 m b

GREEN, William E.
41 01 70 m b
41 02 60 m b
41 03 50 m b
41 04 40 m b
41 05 42 f b
41 06 25 f b
41 07 16 m b
41 08 16 m b
41 09 16 m b
41 10 12 m b
41 11 10 m b
41 12 8 m b
41 13 6 m b
41 14 5 f b
41 15 2 f b

MARTON, Robt. L.
41 01 44 f b
41 02 41 m b
41 03 35 f b
41 04 25 f b
41 05 24 f b
41 06 18 f b
41 07 20 m b
41 08 15 f b
41 09 11 m b
41 10 10 m b
41 11 8 f b
41 12 6 m b
41 13 4 m b
41 14 6 f b
41 15 6 f b
41 16 3 m b
41 17 3 f b
41 18 6/12 m b
41 19 8/12 f b
41 20 6 m b
41 21 4 m b

RANSON, Agness
41 01 29 f b
41 02 79 m b
41 03 5 m b
41 04 3 f b

ESKRIDGE, B. L.
41 01 60 f b

MORGAN, Capt. Joseph
41 01 60 m b
41 02 60 m b
41 03 38 m b
41 04 38 m b
41 05 33 m b
41 06 33 m b
41 07 30 m b
41 08 22 m b
41 09 25 m b
41 10 22 m b
41 11 18 m b
41 12 17 m b
41 13 15 m b
41 14 11 m b
41 15 8 m b
41 16 10 m b
41 17 7 m b
41 18 7 m b
41 19 10 m b
41 20 7 m b
41 21 5 m b

41	22	5	m	b
41	23	2	m	b
41	24	2	m	b
41	25	7	m	b
41	26	3	m	b
41	27	5	m	b
41	28	66	m	b
41	29	60	f	b
41	30	58	f	b
41	31	56	f	b
41	32	48	f	b
41	33	35	f	b
41	34	16	f	b
41	35	30	f	b
41	36	16	f	b
41	37	?	f	b
42	38	23	f	b
42	39	25	f	b
42	40	32	f	b
42	41	30	f	b
42	42	50	f	b
42	43	18	f	b
42	44	30	f	b
42	45	16	f	b
42	46	32	f	b
42	47	8	f	b
42	48	6	f	b
42	49	6	f	b
42	50	3	f	b
42	51	6	f	b
42	52	2	f	b
42	53	2	f	b

MORGAN, Joseph

42	01	65	f	b
42	02	28	f	b
42	03	20	f	b
42	04	16	f	b
42	05	1	f	b
42	06	6	f	b
42	07	5	m	b
42	08	3	m	b
42	09	1	m	m
42	10	60	m	b
42	11	55	m	b
42	12	30	m	b
42	13	26	m	b
42	14	22	m	b
42	15	16	m	b
42	16	14	m	b
42	17	46	m	b
42	18	45	m	b
42	19	60	f	b
42	20	55	f	b
42	21	35	f	b
42	22	30	f	b
42	23	1	m	b

WHITLEY, William J.

42	01	60	f	b
42	02	35	m	b
42	03	13	m	b

EASOM, Susan

42	01	60	m	b
42	02	14	m	b
42	03	12	m	b
42	04	2	m	b
42	05	1	m	b
42	06	1	m	b
42	07	37	f	b
42	08	55	f	b
42	09	14	f	b
42	10	13	f	b
42	11	12	f	b
42	12	7	f	b
42	13	6	f	b

FINKS, Elijah

42	01	60	m	b
42	02	7	m	b

GORDEN, Welington

42	01	40	m	b
42	02	30	m	b
42	03	25	m	b
42	04	12	m	b
42	05	10	m	b
42	06	45	f	b
42	07	40	f	b
42	08	20	f	b
42	09	25	f	b
42	10	25	f	b
42	11	8	f	b
42	12	6	f	b
42	13	5	f	b
42	14	1	f	b
42	15	3	m	b
42	16	2	m	b
42	17	1	m	b
42	18	17	m	b

BOWEN, Harriett M.				
42	01	30	f	m
42	02	35	f	b
42	03	26	f	b
42	04	18	f	m
42	05	25	m	b
42	06	18	m	b
42	07	12	m	m
42	08	7	f	m
43	09	4	f	m
43	10	1	m	m
43	11	6/12	m	m
43	12	6	f	b
WOOD, Jno.				
43	01	40	m	b
43	02	22	m	b
43	03	21	m	b
43	04	22	m	b
43	05	10	f	b
43	06	8	m	b
43	07	2	m	b
43	08	9/12	f	b
PAYNE, Capt. James				
43	01	80	f	b
43	02	75	f	b
43	03	58	f	b
43	04	54	f	b
43	05	45	f	b
43	06	30	f	b
43	07	25	f	b
43	08	17	f	b
43	09	14	f	b
43	10	10	f	b
43	11	5	f	b
43	12	3	f	b
43	13	2	f	b
43	14	40	m	b
43	15	35	m	b
43	16	25	m	b
43	17	24	m	b
43	18	23	m	b
43	19	22	m	b
43	20	14	m	b
43	21	12	m	b
43	22	40	m	b
43	23	22	m	b
43	24	17	m	b
43	25	16	f	b
STONE, Margarett				
43	01	80	f	b
43	02	70	f	b
43	03	18	f	b
43	04	14	f	b
PAYNE, Marshall K.				
43	01	36	m	b
43	02	35	f	b
43	03	11	m	b
HAWLY, George W.				
43	01	10	f	b
KEMPER, Jno.				
43	01	23	f	m
43	02	5	f	m
43	03	2	f	m
43	04	6/12	f	m
ANDERSON, Thomas				
43	01	57	m	b
KELLY, James W.				
43	01	75	m	b
43	02	60	m	b
43	03	50	m	b
43	04	45	m	b
43	05	23	m	b
43	06	22	m	b
43	07	17	m	b
43	08	30	m	b
43	09	28	m	b
43	10	10	m	b
43	11	6	m	b
43	12	1	m	b
43	13	64	m	b
43	14	55	f	b
43	15	45	f	b
43	16	36	f	b
43	17	21	f	b
43	18	20	f	b
43	19	16	f	m
43	20	10	f	b
43	21	8	f	b
43	22	7	f	b
43	23	4	f	b
43	24	7	f	b
43	25	4	f	b
43	26	1	f	b
43	27	13	f	b
43	28	35	m	b
HUMPHRY, Benj'a.				

43 01 39 f b
EMONS, Founton
43 01 17 f b
WEADON, Thomas W.
43 01 59 f b
43 02 39 f b
43 03 27 f b
44 04 19 m b
44 05 14 m b
44 06 11 f b
44 07 10 f b
44 08 9 m b
44 09 7 m b
44 10 5 m b
44 11 5 m b
44 12 3 f b
KEMPER, Capt. George
44 01 43 f b
44 02 15 f b
44 03 15 m b
44 04 13 m b
44 05 12 m b
44 06 10 f b
44 07 5 m b
44 08 4 f b
KEMPER, Henry F.
44 01 65 f b
44 02 50 f b
44 03 65 m b
44 04 35 f b
44 05 22 m b
44 06 12 m b
44 07 16 f b
44 08 15 f b
44 09 8 m b
44 10 8 m b
44 11 10 m b
44 12 1 f b
44 13 8/12 m b
McCONKEY, William
44 01 55 f b
44 02 40 f b
44 03 18 f b
44 04 12 f b
44 05 8 f b
HORTON, Isaac
44 01 39 f b
44 02 34 m b
44 03 5 m b
44 04 2 f b
EMBRY, Jno. J.
44 01 16 f b
MARTON, Lenord
44 01 80 m b
44 02 25 f b
44 03 16 m m
44 04 9 f b
44 05 5 f b
44 06 1 f m
EMBRY, Ro
44 01 64 f b
44 02 30 m m
44 03 23 m b
44 04 23 f m
44 05 15 m b
44 06 12 m b
44 07 10 f b
44 08 8 m m
44 09 7 m b
44 10 7 m b
44 11 5 f m
44 12 4 f b
44 13 3 f b
EMBRY, Oswell P.
44 01 15 f b
ESKRIDGE, Meredith
44 01 60 m b
44 02 40 f b
44 03 35 f b
44 04 25 f b
44 05 22 m b
44 06 22 m b
44 07 19 m b
44 08 18 m b
44 09 16 f b
44 10 14 m b
44 11 14 f b
44 12 13 f b
44 13 12 f b
44 14 8 f b
44 15 6 m b
44 16 5 m b
44 17 12 m b
MARSHALL, Elizabeth N.
44 01 65 m b
44 02 40 f b

44 03 20 m b
44 04 14 f b
44 05 14 m b
44 06 13 m b
44 07 10 f b
45 08 8 f b
45 09 6 m b
45 10 5 m b
45 11 3 m b

STONE, Isaac S.

45 01 70 f b
45 02 61 f b
45 03 40 m b
45 04 30 f b
45 05 25 f b
45 06 40 f b
45 07 16 f b
45 08 15 m b
45 09 11 f b
45 10 9 m b
45 11 9 m b
45 12 8 m b
45 13 7 m b
45 14 6 f b
45 15 5 f b
45 16 5 f b
45 17 4 m b
45 18 1 m b

EMBRY, Stanton

45 01 14 f b
45 02 30 f b
45 03 45 m b

WALKER, Solomon

45 01 18 f b
45 02 11 f b

JONES, William

45 01 57 m b
45 02 40 f b
45 03 24 f b
45 04 22 f b
45 05 20 f b
45 06 15 f b
45 07 11 m b
45 08 9 f b
45 09 2 f b

EMBRY, Henry A.

45 01 50 m b
45 02 30 f b
45 03 11 f b

JAMES, Martha L.

45 01 54 m b
45 02 40 f b
45 03 14 f b
45 04 21 f b
45 05 11 f b
45 06 7 f b
45 07 5 m b
45 08 2 m b

JONES, Henry

45 01 55 m b
45 02 13 f b

ELLES, Lewis

45 01 60 m b
45 02 46 m b
45 03 45 m b
45 04 30 m b
45 05 28 m b
45 06 26 m b
45 07 25 m b
45 08 18 m b
45 09 17 m b
45 10 15 m b
45 11 31 m b
45 12 30 m b
45 13 46 f b
45 14 45 f b
45 15 40 f b
45 16 12 f b
45 17 10 f b
45 18 3 f b

EMBRY, Fredrick

45 01 16 f b

PHILLIPS, Capt. Thomas

45 01 40 f m
45 02 20 f m
45 03 12 f m

Orange Grove Mining Co.

45 01 60 m b
45 02 40 m b
45 03 35 m b
45 04 35 m b
45 05 33 m b
45 06 30 m b
45 07 27 m b
45 08 25 m b
45 09 20 m b

45	10	21	m	b
45	11	18	m	b
45	12	16	m	b
45	13	15	m	b
46	14	16	m	b
46	15	17	m	b
46	16	18	m	b
46	17	25	m	b
46	18	25	m	b
46	19	15	m	b
46	20	5	m	b
46	21	30	f	b

ROYAL, Jno. J.

46	01	44	m	b
46	02	28	m	b
46	03	20	m	b
46	04	44	f	b
46	05	40	f	b
46	06	19	f	b
46	07	10	m	b
46	08	8	m	b
46	09	6	m	b
46	10	4	m	b
46	11	2	m	b

SKINKER, Harriett

46	01	80	m	b
46	02	78	m	b
46	03	71	m	b
46	04	65	m	b
46	05	48	m	b
46	06	40	m	m
46	07	53	m	b
46	08	25	m	b
46	09	21	m	b
46	10	50	m	m
46	11	22	m	b
46	12	13	m	b
46	13	12	m	m
46	14	11	m	b
46	15	12	m	b
46	16	9	m	b
46	17	8	m	m
46	18	4	m	m
46	19	65	f	b
46	20	45	f	b
46	21	41	f	b
46	22	35	f	b
46	23	40	f	b
46	24	55	f	b
46	25	33	f	b
46	26	21	f	b
46	27	17	f	m
46	28	7	f	b
46	29	6	f	b
46	30	2	f	m

SHACKLEFORD, Uriah

46	01	14	f	b

HAMES, James S.

46	01	84	f	b
46	02	47	m	b
46	03	45	f	b
46	04	14	f	b

STRINGFELLOW, Hannah

46	01	70	f	b
46	02	45	f	b
46	03	50	f	m
46	04	23	f	b
46	05	15	f	b
46	06	8	f	b
46	07	7	f	b
46	08	5	f	m
46	09	10	f	m
46	10	50	m	b
46	11	17	m	b
46	12	13	m	b
46	13	11	m	m
46	14	4	m	b
46	15	3	m	b
46	16	1	m	m
46	17	1	m	b
46	18	9/12	m	m

EMBRY, William

46	01	75	f	b
46	02	21	m	b
46	03	20	m	b
46	04	18	m	b
46	05	14	f	b
46	06	8	f	b
46	07	30	m	b
46	08	21	m	b

SKINKER, S. W.

46	01	60	f	b
46	02	40	m	b
46	03	30	f	b
46	04	25	f	b
47	05	23	f	b

47 06 22 f b
47 07 20 m b
47 08 19 f b
47 09 14 m b
47 10 60 m b
47 11 10 m b
47 12 9 m b
47 13 11 f b
47 14 5 m b
47 15 6 f b
47 16 2 f b
47 17 2 f b
47 18 3 m b
47 19 1 m b
47 20 2 m b

EMBRY, William
47 01 65 m b
47 02 66 f b
47 03 41 f b
47 04 40 m b
47 05 20 f b
47 06 19 f b
47 07 20 m b
47 08 16 m b
47 09 15 f b
47 10 14 f b
47 11 10 m b
47 12 6 m b
47 13 5 f b
47 14 3 f b
47 15 1 f b
47 16 1 f b

EMBRY, Lieucinder
47 01 55 m b
47 02 25 m b
47 03 17 m b
47 04 12 m b
47 05 2 m b
47 06 40 f b
47 07 18 f b
47 08 14 f b
47 09 13 f b
47 10 11 f b
47 11 6 f b
47 12 4 f b
47 13 7/12 f b

OLIVER, Joel
47 01 15 f b
47 02 14 f b

EMBRY, Arthor
47 01 14 f b

OLIVER, Charles A.
47 01 20 f b
47 02 1 f b

JONES, Alexander T.
47 01 60 f b
47 02 50 m b
47 03 13 m b
47 04 12 f b

CALBERT, Ann
47 01 30 f b
47 02 18 f b
47 03 4 f b
47 04 1 m b

COOPPER, Doct. W. D.
47 01 57 f b
47 02 14 m b
47 03 6 f b

BLACKWELL, Hannah R.
47 01 48 f b
47 02 43 f b
47 03 27 f m
47 04 25 m b
47 05 13 m b
47 06 10 m b
47 07 9 f b
47 08 10 m b
47 09 8 m b
47 10 6 f b
47 11 5 f b
47 12 4 m b
47 13 2 f b

ALLEN, Capt. Landon
47 01 14 m b
47 02 30 f b
47 03 10 m b
47 04 8 f b
47 05 3 m b
47 06 9/12 f b

PETTEY, Charles
47 01 20 f b
47 02 14 f b

McLEAREN, Capt. James
47 01 20 f b
47 02 4 m b
48 03 45 f b

48 04 5 m b
BENNETT, William
48 01 30 f b
48 02 20 f b
48 03 18 f b
48 04 16 m b
48 05 14 f b
48 06 12 m b
48 07 4 m b
48 08 8 m b
48 09 9 f b
48 10 6 f b
48 11 6 m b
48 12 4 m b
48 13 4 f b
48 14 3 f b
48 15 6/12 f b
SOTHARD, James
48 01 55 f b
48 02 45 m b
48 03 19 m b
48 04 9 f b
EDWARDS, Benj'a.
48 01 55 m b
OLIVER, Granville J.
48 01 50 f b
48 02 49 f b
48 03 28 f b
48 04 16 m b
48 05 14 m b
48 06 10 m b
48 07 8 f b
48 08 6 f b
48 09 3 f b
THORN, Jno.
48 01 17 f b
48 02 8 m b
48 03 7 f b
48 04 6 m b
48 05 5 f b
RECTOR, Elias
48 01 22 f b
RECTOR, Joel
48 01 9 m b
OLIVER, Nancy
48 01 10 m b
EMBRY, Thomas M.
48 01 19 f b
48 02 13 m b
48 03 1 f b
EUSTACE, Sarah M.
48 01 50 m b
CRUMP, George
48 01 34 m b
48 02 32 f b
48 03 32 f b
48 04 14 m b
48 05 13 m b
48 06 10 f b
48 07 7 f b
48 08 5 f b
48 09 4 f b
48 10 4 f b
48 11 2 m b
GEORGE, Alithea
48 01 50 m b
48 02 50 f b
48 03 45 f b
48 04 25 f b
48 05 24 f b
48 06 23 f b
48 07 23 f b
48 08 21 f b
48 09 18 f b
48 10 17 f b
48 11 21 f b
48 12 14 f b
48 13 10 f b
48 14 6 f b
48 15 4 f b
48 16 3 f b
48 17 8/12 f b
48 18 6/12 f b
48 19 29 m b
48 20 15 m b
48 21 14 m b
48 22 16 m b
48 23 12 m b
48 24 11 m b
48 25 4 m b
48 26 2 m b
48 27 1 m b
48 28 6/12 m b
CROPP, Silas F.
48 01 60 f b
48 02 50 f b

49 03 50 m b
49 04 40 m b
49 05 22 m b
49 06 14 m b
49 07 12 m b
49 08 10 m b
49 09 7 m b
49 10 3 m b
49 11 2 m b
49 12 25 f b
49 13 23 f b
49 14 22 f b
49 15 21 f b
49 16 20 f b
49 17 10 f b
49 18 4 m b
49 19 5 m b
49 20 4 f b
49 21 8/12 f b
49 22 8/12 f b

EUSTACE, William H.

49 01 30 f b
49 02 8 f b
49 03 5 f b
49 04 3 f b
49 05 7/12 f b
49 06 14 m b

HANSBOROUGH, Jno.

49 01 35 m b
49 02 18 m b
49 03 21 f b
49 04 1 m b
49 05 13 f b

BLACKWELL, Elizabeth

49 01 65 m b
49 02 55 m m
49 03 36 m m
49 04 27 m m
49 05 25 m m
49 06 14 m m
49 07 13 m m
49 08 12 m m
49 09 9 m m
49 10 5 m m
49 11 6 m m
49 12 9/12 m m
49 13 62 f m
49 14 60 f m
49 15 54 f m
49 16 50 f m
49 17 30 f m
49 18 27 f m
49 19 25 f m
49 20 24 f m
49 21 17 f m
49 22 18 f m
49 23 10 f m
49 24 9 f m
49 25 7 f m
49 26 4 f m
49 27 6 f m *
* idiotic
49 28 5 f m
49 29 5 f m
49 30 1 f m
49 31 1 f m
49 32 3 f m
49 33 2 f m
49 34 9/12 f m

SHOEMAKER, Lewis

49 01 80 f b *
* deaf & blind
49 02 40 f b
49 03 41 f b
49 04 28 f b
49 05 18 f b
49 06 6 f b
49 07 5 f b
49 08 37 m b
49 09 17 m b
49 10 16 m b
49 11 7 m b
49 12 4 m b

BUTLER, Robt.

49 01 8 m b

BOWER, Capt. William

49 01 25 m b
49 02 18 m b
49 03 16 m b
49 04 10 m b
49 05 8 m b
49 06 6 m b
50 07 6 m b
50 08 5 m b
50 09 1 m b
50 10 45 f b

50	11	44	f	b
50	12	43	f	b
50	13	22	f	b
50	14	15	f	b
50	15	12	f	b
50	16	12	f	b

RECTOR, Thompson

50	01	35	f	b
50	02	100	f	m
50	03	6	f	b
50	04	8/12	m	b

HORD, Enos

50	01	56	f	b
50	02	54	f	b
50	03	53	m	b
50	04	57	f	b
50	05	50	f	b
50	06	48	f	b
50	07	40	m	b
50	08	39	f	b
50	09	31	f	b
50	10	30	f	b
50	11	30	f	b
50	12	29	f	b
50	13	27	m	b
50	14	25	f	b
50	15	23	f	b
50	16	23	f	b
50	17	22	f	b
50	18	21	f	b
50	19	20	f	b
50	20	19	m	b
50	22	15	f	b
50	23	14	f	b
50	24	13	f	b
50	25	13	f	b
50	26	12	f	b
50	27	11	f	b
50	28	11	f	b
50	29	11	f	b
50	30	10	f	b
50	31	9	f	b
50	32	9	f	b
50	33	9	m	b
50	34	9	m	b
50	35	8	f	b
50	36	7	m	b
50	37	7	m	b
50	38	6	f	b
50	39	6	f	b
50	40	6	m	b
50	41	5	f	b
50	42	5	f	b
50	43	4	m	b
50	44	4	m	b
50	45	4	f	b
50	46	3	f	b
50	47	3	f	b
50	48	2	m	b
50	49	2	f	b
50	50	2	m	b
50	51	1	m	b
50	52	1	m	b
50	53	1	f	b
50	54	1	f	b
50	55	1	m	b
50	56	1	m	b
50	57	9/12	m	b
50	58	9/12	f	b
50	59	8/12	f	b
50	60	8/12	m	b
50	61	9/12	m	b

JONES, James S.

50	01	45	m	b
50	02	10	f	b
50	03	7	m	b

PILCHER, Daniel

50	01	41	f	b
50	02	25	f	b
50	03	20	f	b
50	04	12	m	b
50	05	10	m	b
50	06	8	m	b
50	07	4	f	b
51	08	3	f	b
51	09	3	m	b
51	10	6	m	b

BEALE, Jno. G.

51	01	55	m	b
51	02	40	m	b
51	03	39	m	b
51	04	35	m	b
51	05	33	m	b
51	06	50	m	b
51	07	27	m	b
51	08	29	m	b

51 09 28 m b
51 10 27 m b
51 11 26 m b
51 12 25 m b
51 12 25 m b
51 13 24 m b
51 14 24 m b
51 15 23 m b
51 16 24 m b
51 17 22 m b
51 18 20 m b
51 19 19 m b
51 20 16 m b
51 21 10 m b
51 22 9 m b
51 23 9 m b
51 24 8 m b
51 25 7 m b
51 26 6 m b
51 27 5 m b
51 28 5 m b
51 29 4 m b
51 30 4 m b
51 31 4 m b
51 32 3 m b
51 33 3 m b
51 34 3 m b
51 35 40 f b
51 36 40 f b
51 37 39 f b
51 38 39 f b
51 39 30 f b
51 40 29 f b
51 41 28 f b
51 42 27 f b
51 43 26 f b
51 44 25 f b
51 45 24 f b
51 46 23 f b
51 47 22 f b
51 48 21 f b
51 49 12 f b
51 50 11 f b
51 51 10 f b
51 52 9 f b
51 53 8 f b
51 54 7 f b
51 55 6 f b
51 56 5 f b
51 57 4 f b
51 58 3 f b
51 59 2 f b

JAMES, Elizabeth B.

51 01 68 m b
51 02 67 m b
51 03 55 m b
51 04 34 m b
51 05 22 m b
51 06 5 m b
51 07 5 m b
51 08 5 m b *

* deformed

51 09 68 f b
51 10 50 f b
51 11 48 f b
51 12 34 f b
51 13 20 f b
51 14 14 f b
51 15 10 f b
51 16 9 f b
51 17 8 f b
51 18 7 f b
51 19 6 f b

RANDOLPH, Charles

51 01 59 m b
51 02 58 m b
52 03 48 m b
52 04 47 m b
52 05 46 m b
52 06 46 m b
52 07 40 m b
52 08 40 m b
52 09 39 m b
52 10 35 m b
52 11 34 m b
52 12 16 m b
52 13 15 m b
52 14 16 m b
52 15 13 m b
52 16 12 m b
52 17 12 m b
52 18 11 m b
52 19 70 f b
52 20 48 f b
52 21 56 f b
52 22 45 f b

52 23 44 f b
52 24 53 f b
52 25 26 f b
52 26 33 f b
52 27 40 f b
52 28 35 f b
52 29 14 f b
52 30 13 f b
52 31 15 f b
52 32 11 f b
52 33 9 f b
52 34 9 f b
52 35 8 f b
52 36 9 f b
52 37 6 f b
52 38 5 m b
52 39 4 f b
52 40 3 f b
52 41 1 m b
52 42 4 f b
52 43 1 f b

SINCLAIR, Rosamond

52 01 97 f m *
* blind
52 02 80 m b
52 03 65 m b
52 04 60 f b
52 05 55 m b
52 06 50 m b
52 07 48 m b
52 08 30 m b
52 09 30 m b
52 10 28 f b
52 11 28 f m
52 12 26 f m
52 13 26 f b
52 14 23 f b
52 15 22 f b
52 16 20 f b
52 17 19 f b
52 18 17 m b
52 19 11 f b
52 20 10 f b
52 21 10 m b
52 22 9 m b
52 23 8 f b
52 24 7 m b
52 25 8 m b
52 26 8 f b
52 27 13 m b *
* deaf & dumb
52 28 8 m b
52 29 8 m b
52 30 7 m b
52 31 4 f b
52 32 4 f b
52 33 5 m b
52 34 5 f b
52 35 1 m b
52 36 1 m m
52 37 53 f b

ROBBERSON, Samuel

52 01 28 f b
52 02 24 m b
52 03 24 m b
52 04 18 f b
52 05 10 f b

MARTON, Mary

53 01 65 m b
53 02 32 m b
53 03 18 m b
53 04 9 m b
53 05 2 m b
53 06 50 f b
53 07 30 f m
53 08 11 f m
53 09 5 f b
53 10 8 f b
53 11 9/12 f b

FICKLIN, William P.

53 01 65 m b
53 02 58 m b
53 03 25 m b
53 04 22 m b
53 05 16 m b
53 06 15 m b
53 07 12 m b
53 08 9 m b
53 09 8 m b
53 10 7 m b
53 11 5 m b
53 12 4 m b
53 13 2 m b
53 14 100 f m
53 15 31 f b
53 16 28 f b

53	17	20	f	b
53	18	30	f	m
53	19	28	f	b
53	20	12	f	b
53	21	10	f	b
53	22	8	f	b
53	23	6	f	b
53	24	2	f	b
53	24	2	f	b

JOHNSON, Thomas T.

53	01	72	f	b
53	02	50	f	b
53	03	50	f	b
53	04	16	f	b
53	05	14	f	b
53	06	10	f	b
53	07	8	f	b
53	08	42	m	b
53	09	40	m	b
53	10	28	m	b
53	11	21	m	b
53	12	16	m	b

JOHNSON, George A.

53	01	4	m	b
53	02	26	f	b
53	03	4	m	b

FICKLIN, Guss

53	01	65	f	b
53	02	36	m	b
53	03	35	m	b
53	04	25	f	b
53	05	11	f	b
53	06	12	m	b
53	07	8	m	b
53	08	8	m	b

PORTER, Betsy

53	01	9	m	b

MARTIN, Jno.

53	01	30	f	b
53	02	22	f	b
53	03	18	f	b
53	04	7	f	b
53	05	3	f	b
53	06	31	m	b
53	07	12	m	b
53	08	10	m	b
53	09	5	m	b
53	10	4	m	b

HOL[T]SCLAW, Nancy

53	01	40	f	b
53	02	10	f	b
53	03	8	m	b
53	04	1	m	b

BURSEY, William H.

53	01	30	m	b
53	02	14	m	b
53	03	35	f	b
53	04	25	f	b
53	05	7	m	b
53	06	3	m	b
53	07	1	f	b

KELLEY, Dinah

53	01	50	m	n
53	02	36	f	b
53	03	33?	f	m
54	04	20	f	b
54	05	18	m	b
54	06	14	m	b
54	07	9	m	b
54	08	12	f	b
54	09	8	m	b
54	10	6	m	b
54	11	4	f	b
54	12	4	f	b
54	13	2	f	b
54	14	1	f	b

BEAL, Doct. Jno. G.

54	01	49	f	b
54	02	25	f	b
54	03	22	m	b
54	04	15	f	b
54	05	12	m	b
54	06	11	m	b
54	07	4	f	b
54	08	2	f	b

SHOEMAKE [SHUMATE], Lewis

54	01	70	m	b	
54	02	60	m	b	*
		* fugitive?			
54	03	45	m	b	
54	04	25	m	b	
54	05	20	m	b	
54	06	15	m	b	
54	07	45	f	b	
54	08	20	f	b	
54	09	13	f	b	

54 10 12 f b
54 11 6 f b
54 12 2 f b

FISHER, Capt. Thomas

54 01 60 f b
54 02 27 f b
54 03 26 f b
54 04 25 f b
54 06 24 f b
54 07 12 f b
54 08 6 f b
54 09 5 f b
54 10 4 f b
54 11 2 f b
54 12 60 m b
54 13 40 m b
54 14 30 m b
54 15 28 m b
54 16 26 m b
54 17 18 m b
54 18 15 m b
54 19 13 m b
54 20 13 m b
54 21 11 m b
54 22 9 m b
54 23 8 m b
54 24 6 m b
54 25 6 m b
54 26 4 m b

FLETCHER, Alexandra

54 01 10 m b

HEFLIN, William

54 01 40 m b
54 02 20 m b
54 03 4 m b
54 04 4 m b
54 05 3 m b
54 06 2 m b
54 07 25 f b
54 08 22 f b
54 09 6 f b
54 10 2 f b

STUART, Nancy

54 01 50 m b
54 02 30 f b
54 03 10 m b
54 04 6 m b
54 05 6 f b
54 06 4 f b
54 07 2 m b
54 08 9/12 m b

PAGETT, Dempsey

54 01 43 f b
54 02 19 f b
54 03 17 f b
54 04 10 f b
54 05 24 m b
54 06 23 m b
54 07 16 m b
54 08 50 m b

HAWLEY, Henry S.

55 01 57 m b
55 02 49 f b
55 03 19 f b
55 04 12 m b
55 05 4 m b
55 06 14 m b

MINTER, William J.

55 01 22 f b
55 02 1 f b

CANER, Jno

55 01 50 m b

STROTHER, James

55 01 55 f b
55 02 28 m b
55 03 27 f b
55 04 20 m b
55 05 16 f m
55 06 12 f b
55 07 6 m b
55 08 2 m b

STRIBBLING, Doct. R. M.

55 01 80 m b
55 02 70 f b
55 03 40 f m
55 04 40 f m
55 05 35 f b
55 06 30 f b
55 07 30 m m
55 08 22 m b
55 09 22 m m
55 10 16 f m
55 11 15 m m
55 12 12 m m
55 13 10 f m
55 14 6 f m

55 15 16 f m
55 16 14 f m
55 17 6 f m
55 18 4 f m
55 19 2 f m
55 20 12 f m
55 21 10 f b
55 22 8 f b
55 23 6 m b
55 24 4 f b
55 25 2 f b
55 26 13 m b
55 27 11 m b
55 28 9 m b
55 29 7 m b
55 30 5 m b
55 31 6/12 m b

ANDERSON, Daniel
55 01 35 f b
55 02 14 f b

KIRBY, Jno. G.
55 01 26 m b
55 02 12 f b

KIRBY, William H.
55 01 16 f m

MITCHEL, James
55 01 45 f b

HORNER, Doct. Fredrick
55 01 50 f b
55 02 24 f b
55 03 13 m b
55 04 11 m b
55 05 4 f b
55 06 6/12 f m

BRAGG, Charles
55 01 40 m m
55 02 25 m m
55 03 23 m b
55 04 19 m b
55 05 23 m b
55 06 30 f m
55 07 29 f m
55 08 15 f b
55 09 20 m b

SMITH, Jno.
55 01 43 m b
55 02 28 m m
55 03 22 m b
55 04 17 m b
55 05 13 m b *
* blind
55 06 30 f b
55 07 48 f b
55 08 40 f b
55 09 20 f m
55 10 10 f b

KEMPER, Jno. P.
55 01 9 f m

SANDERS, Alfred
55 01 10 f b

PATTEY, William A.
55 01 45 f b
55 02 9 f b

HELM, Doct. William
55 01 35 f b
56 02 30 f m
56 03 14 m m
56 04 10 m m
56 05 6 m b
56 06 1 m b

CARTER, Henry L.
56 01 27 f b
56 02 18 f b

BOOTH, George
56 01 15 f b

FRANKLIN, Ann E.
56 01 45 f b

ADAMS, Lucy
56 01 47 f b

TOPLETT, George W.
56 01 15 f b
56 02 13 m b

FINKS, Jno. W.
56 01 40 f m
56 02 50 m b
56 03 16 m m
56 04 13 f b

MOCKLY, William
56 01 30 f m

FINKS, Thomas
56 01 12 f b
56 02 26 f b

BROOK, James V.
56 01 30 f b
56 02 13 f b
56 03 11 f m

GRANT, Jno. M.
56 01 26 m b
56 02 30 m m
56 03 25 f b
56 04 64 f b
56 05 10 f m
56 06 20 m m
CROSS, Cyrus
56 01 33 f b
56 02 12 f b
RINSBURG, Abraham
56 01 12 f b
56 02 9 f b
RICHARD, Alexander
56 01 50 f b
BECKHAM, Jno. G.
56 01 55 m b
56 02 20 m b
56 03 15 m b
56 04 12 m b
56 05 23 f b
56 06 22 f b
56 07 4 f b
56 08 1 m b
56 09 25 m b
56 10 25 m b
56 11 20 m b
NICKSON, Rev'd. R. T.
56 01 40 f b
56 02 12 f m
AUSTON, Doct. James
56 01 40 m b
56 02 26 f b
56 03 14 m m
56 04 12 f m
BROOK, Ann
56 01 60 m b
56 02 35 m b
56 03 17 m b
56 04 15 m b
56 05 10 m b
56 06 7 m m
56 07 6 m b
56 08 5 m m
56 09 5 m b
56 10 52 f b
56 11 50 f b
56 12 56 f b
56 13 18 f m
56 14 9/12 f m
ROB, Sarah
56 01 23 f b
56 02 1 f b
56 03 17 f m
56 04 60 f b
NORRIS, William C.
56 01 60 m b
56 02 55 f m
56 03 32 f b
56 04 30 f m
56 05 11 f m
56 06 7 m b
56 07 7 m b
56 08 1 m b
56 09 1 m b
SHIPP, Lucy B.
56 01 60 m b
56 02 40 m b
56 03 50 m b
56 04 45 f b
56 05 15 f b
56 06 10 f b
56 07 7 m b
57 08 4 m b
CHILTON, Samuel
57 01 70 f b
57 02 25 f b
57 03 17 f b
MARR, Catharine J.
57 01 35 f b
57 02 12 f m
57 03 7 m b
57 04 9 f b
SMITH, Richard M.
57 01 40 m b
57 02 16 m b
57 03 10 m b
57 04 40 f b
57 05 35 f b
57 06 34 f b
57 07 30 f b
57 08 5 f b
57 09 4 m b
PAYNE, Richard
57 01 41 f b
57 02 30 m b

57 03 25 f b
57 04 16 m b
57 05 5 m b
57 06 4 f b
57 07 13 f b
57 08 65 m b

DICKSON, Henry T.
57 01 65 f b

MANYETT, Antone
57 01 28 m m

GORDEN, Robt.
57 01 60 f b
57 02 33 m b
57 03 17 m b
57 04 25 m b
57 05 16 m b
57 06 11 m m
57 07 11 f b

WOODEN, William
57 01 12 f b

FISHER, Doct. Samuel B.
57 01 29 f b
57 02 28 f m
57 03 27 f m
57 04 30 f m
57 05 50 m m
57 06 50 m b
57 07 12 m m
57 08 12 f b
57 09 10 f m
57 10 8 f m
57 11 7 m m
57 12 7 m m
57 13 6 m m
57 14 9 m m
57 15 4 m m
57 16 6 f b
57 17 4 f b
57 18 2 m b
57 19 4 f m
57 20 3 f m
57 21 6/12 f b
57 22 6/12 f b
57 23 40 f b
57 24 5 f b
57 25 5 f b

SMITH, Elizabeth
57 01 65 f b
57 02 55 f b
57 03 50 f b
57 04 17 f b
57 05 ? f b
57 06 19 m b
57 07 17 m b

HAMES, Alice A.
57 01 28 f m
57 02 6 f b
57 03 4 m b
57 04 1 m b
57 05 7 f b

JOHNSON, William
57 01 55 f b
57 02 14 f m
57 03 4 f b
57 04 2 m b

FANT, Jno. L.
57 01 50 m b
57 02 49 m b
57 03 30 m b
57 04 20 m b
57 05 45 m b
57 06 12 m b
57 07 11 m b
58 08 65 f b
58 09 60 f b
58 10 25 f b
58 11 20 f b
58 12 12 f b

MECKLY, Jno. W.
58 01 26 f m
58 02 11 f m
58 03 1 f m

JENNINGS, William H.
58 01 40 f b
58 02 24 m b
58 03 10 f b

DAY, Baldwin
58 01 55 m b
58 02 45 m b
58 03 35 m b
58 04 21 m b
58 05 5 m b
58 06 3 m b
58 07 1 m b
58 08 24 f b
58 09 23 f b

58 10 23 f b
58 11 4 f b
58 12 2 f b
58 13 9/12 f b

FOLLIN, Maddison J.
58 01 63 m b
58 02 20 f b
58 03 16 f b
58 04 15 f b
58 04 15 f b

BACKRACK, Jacob
58 01 14 f b

COLOGN, Vinston
58 01 55 f b

COLOGN, Edgar M.
58 01 55 f b
58 02 15 m b
58 03 11 f b

ROSS, Jno.
58 01 35 f b
58 02 8 f b

CASH, Lucy Y.
58 01 8 f m

SANDERS, Jno. M.
58 01 45 m b
58 02 28 f b
58 03 12 f m
58 04 9 f b
58 05 7 m b
58 06 6 m b
58 07 2 m b

WILLIAMS, Elias
58 01 50 f b
58 02 12 f b

ENGLISH, Elizabeth
58 01 65 f b
58 02 45 f b
58 03 60 m b
58 04 20 f b
58 05 12 f b

TONG, Jno. R.
58 01 53 m b
58 02 20 m b
58 03 19 f b
58 04 28 f b
58 05 12 m b
58 06 6 f b
58 07 4 f b

TYLOR, Jno. W.
58 01 53 m b
58 02 45 f m
58 03 50 f m
58 04 20 f b
58 05 18 f m
58 06 12 f b
58 07 10 m m
58 08 8/12 f m
58 09 35 m b

BILL, William
58 01 65 f b
58 02 64 m b
58 03 50 m b
58 04 50 m b
58 05 40 f b
58 06 25 f b
58 07 24 f b
58 08 35 m b
58 09 12 f b
58 10 14 m b
58 11 3 m b
58 12 4 m b
58 13 3 m b
58 14 2 m b
58 15 30 f b
58 16 7 f b
58 17 3 f b
58 18 2 f b
59 19 7/12 m b

COOPPER, Richard
59 01 35 f b
59 02 5 m b
59 03 10 m m

JENNINGS, Lucy
59 01 65 m b
59 02 65 f b
59 03 50 f b
59 04 14 f b

WHITE, H. A.
59 01 30 f m
59 02 20 f m
59 03 15 f m
59 04 2 f m
59 05 28 m m
59 06 7 m m
59 07 7 m m
59 08 45 m b

PHILLIPS, Col. Wm. F.

59	01	55	f	b
59	02	23	f	b
59	03	25	m	m
59	04	8	f	b
59	05	3	f	b

JOHNSON, Phill S.

59	01	45	m	b
59	02	40	m	b
59	03	18	m	b
59	04	19	m	b
59	05	8	m	b
59	06	6	m	b
59	07	4	m	b
59	08	19	f	b
59	09	18	f	b
59	10	16	f	b
59	11	12?	f	b
59	12	10	f	b

POLLOCK, Parson D. A.

59	01	50	f	b
59	02	35	f	b
59	03	18	f	b
59	04	16	f	b
59	05	16	m	b
59	06	12	m	b
59	07	10	m	b
59	08	8	m	b
59	09	50	m	b
59	10	50	m	b
59	11	23	m	b
59	12	30	m	b
59	13	25	m	b
59	14	20	f	b
59	15	7	f	b
59	16	20	f	b

LEOR, James

59	01	85	m	m
59	02	50	m	b
59	03	50	m	b
59	04	25	m	b
59	05	85	f	b
59	06	40	f	b
59	07	12	f	b
59	08	10	m	b
59	09	7	m	b
59	10	30	m	b
59	11	40	m	b
59	12	55	m	b

PUTMAN, Bartimus

59	01	20	f	b

KEMPER, Charles

59	01	55	f	b
59	02	35	f	b
59	03	31	m	b
59	04	30	f	b
59	05	29	f	b
59	06	36	m	b
59	07	26	m	b
59	08	18	f	b
59	09	24	m	b
59	10	19	m	b
59	11	14	m	b
59	12	11	f	b
59	13	9	m	b
59	14	32	f	b
59	15	28	f	b
59	16	25	f	b
59	17	8	f	b
59	18	8	f	b
59	19	5	m	b
59	20	5	f	b
59	21	1	m	b
59	22	1	f	b
60	23	1	f	b
60	24	1	f	b
60	25	48	m	b

BASHAW, Elijah

60	01	59	f	b	
60	02	59	m	b	
60	03	34	f	b	
60	04	32	f	b	
60	05	18	m	b	
60	06	15	m	b	
60	07	18	f	m	
60	08	13	m	m	
60	09	13	f	b	
60	10	9	f	m	
60	11	7	f	b	
60	12	7	f	m	
60	13	4	m	b	
60	14	9/12	m	b	*

* idiotic & blind

BARROW, Jno. D.

60	01	45	m	b
60	02	44	m	b

60 03 35 m b
60 04 36 m b
60 05 16 m b
60 06 12 m b
60 07 11 m b
60 08 13 m b
60 09 10 m b
60 10 10 m b
60 11 10 m b
60 12 42 f b
60 13 40 f b
60 14 15 f b
60 15 12 f b
60 16 11 f b
60 17 2 f b
60 18 9/12 f b
60 19 9/12 m b
60 20 17 f b
60 21 16 f b
60 22 9 f b
60 23 7 f b
60 24 4 f b
60 25 37 f b
60 26 7 f b
60 27 5 f b
60 28 4 m b
60 29 9/12 m b

HOLTZCLAW, William

60 01 45 m b
60 02 33 m b
60 03 59 m b
60 04 27 m b
60 05 28 m b
60 06 20 m b
60 07 16 m b
60 08 15 m b
60 09 35 m b
60 10 10 m b
60 11 8 m b
60 12 7 m b
60 13 5 m b
60 14 4 m b
60 15 2 m b
60 16 3 m b
60 17 4 m b
60 18 80 f b
60 19 40 f b
60 20 35 f b
60 21 7 f b
60 22 5 f b

MARSHALL, Doct. J. A.

60 01 70 m b
60 02 60 m b
60 03 40 m m
60 04 40 m b
60 05 39 m b
60 06 40 m b
60 07 37 m b
60 08 21 m b
60 09 21 m *

* albino

60 10 19 m m
60 11 60 m b
60 12 24 m b
60 13 14 m m
60 14 12 m m
60 15 12 m m
60 16 10 m m
61 17 10 m b
61 18 9 m b
61 19 8 m b
61 20 6 m b
61 21 4 m b
61 22 6 m b
61 23 15 m b
61 24 2 m b
61 25 50 f b
61 26 60 f b
61 27 61 f b
61 28 55 f m
61 29 40 f b
61 30 38 f b
61 31 35 f b
61 32 20 f b
61 33 16 f b
61 34 16 f b
61 35 15 f b
61 36 14 f b
61 37 12 f m
61 38 10 f b
61 39 8 f b
61 40 6 f b
61 41 8 f m
61 42 7/12 f b

RAMY, Thos.

61 01 25 m b

61 02 27 m b
61 03 16 f b
61 04 9/12 f b
61 05 25 m b
61 06 55 m b
61 07 18 f b

MARSHALL, Jno.
61 01 49 m b
61 02 48 m b
61 03 40 f m
61 04 15 m b
61 05 14 f b
61 06 18 f m
61 07 14 m b
61 08 12 f b
61 09 10 m b
61 10 12 f b
61 11 30 f b
61 12 11 m m
61 13 4 m m
61 14 1 m m
61 15 7 f b
61 16 5 m b
61 17 3 f b
61 18 8/12 f b

MARSHALL, Doct. Ashton A.
61 01 25 m b
61 02 25 m b
61 03 44 m b
61 04 23 m b
61 05 22 m b
61 06 18 m b
61 07 17 m b
61 08 20 m b
61 09 50 f b
61 10 26 f b
61 11 15 f b
61 12 5 m b
61 13 3 f b

MARSHALL, James K.
61 01 75 m m
61 02 60 f b
61 03 50 f b
61 04 24 m b
61 05 20 f b
61 06 46 f b
61 07 24 f b
61 08 18 f b
61 09 16 f b
61 10 6 f b
61 11 48 f b
61 12 40 m b
61 13 60 m b
61 14 24 f b
61 15 5 m b
61 16 3 m b
61 17 22 f b
61 18 2 m b
61 19 40 m b
61 20 35 f b
62 21 13 f b
62 22 7 m b
62 23 4 m b
62 24 9/12 f b
62 25 34 f b
62 26 14 f b
62 27 12 f b
62 28 10 m b
62 29 7 f b
62 30 5 m b
62 31 24 f b
62 32 22 f b
62 33 1 f b
62 34 50 m b
62 35 28 f b
62 36 8 m b
62 37 6 m b
62 38 3 f b
62 39 50 f b
62 40 24 m b
62 41 15 f b
62 42 13 f b
62 43 9 m b
62 44 4 f b
62 45 50 f b
62 46 17 f b
62 47 15 f b
62 48 40 f b
62 49 10 f b
62 50 8 f b
62 51 6 f b
62 52 4 m b
62 53 50 m b
62 54 30 m b
62 55 2 f b

RICE, Jno. S. at Marshall

62 01 51 m b
62 02 50 m b
62 03 28 m b
62 04 26 m b
62 05 25 m b
62 06 24 m b
62 07 23 m b
62 08 21 m b
62 09 18 m m
62 10 7 m b
62 11 14 m b
62 12 13 m b
62 13 9 m b
62 14 10 m b
62 15 6 m m
62 16 4 m b
62 17 4 m b
62 18 2 m b
62 19 55 f b
62 20 48 f b
62 21 35 f b
62 22 25 f b
62 23 23 f b
62 24 19 f b
62 25 18 f b
62 26 15 f b
62 27 12 f b
62 28 8 f b
62 29 7 f b
62 30 6 f m
62 31 4 f b
62 32 2 f b
62 33 9/12 f b
62 34 1 f b
62 35 2 f b
62 36 20 m b

RICE, Jno. S.

62 01 70 f b
62 02 70 m b
62 03 46 m b
62 04 45 m b
62 05 58 m b
62 06 23 m b
62 07 18 m b
62 08 20 m m
62 09 26 f b
62 10 6 f b
62 11 4 f b
62 12 2 f b
62 13 14 f b

MARSHALL, Edward C.

63 01 46 f m
63 02 46 f b
63 03 50 f b
63 04 35 f b
63 05 30 f b
63 06 30 f b
63 07 25 f b
63 08 25 f b
63 09 24 f b
63 10 16 f b
63 11 14 f b
63 12 14 f b
63 13 12 f b
63 14 8 f b
63 15 7 f b
63 16 5 f b
63 17 5 f b
63 18 5 f b
63 19 50 m b
63 20 49 m b
63 21 45 m b
63 22 35 m b
63 23 25 m b
63 24 23 m b
63 25 20 m b
63 26 16 m b
63 27 16 m b
63 28 13 m b
63 29 13 m b
63 30 8 m b
63 31 8 m b
63 32 5 m b
63 33 5 m b
63 34 4 m b

SANDERS, William

63 01 60 m b
63 02 17 m b
63 03 53 m b
63 04 23 m b
63 05 26 f b
63 06 8/12 m b

FEAGANS, Benj'a.

63 01 26 m b
63 02 25 m b
63 03 17 f b

63 04 3 f b
63 05 9/12 f b
63 06 50 m b
63 07 40 m b

HALL, Thos. J.
63 01 50 f b
63 02 50 f b
63 03 45 m b
63 04 24 m m
63 05 26 m m

ANDERSON, E. M.
63 01 60 m b
63 02 50 f b
63 03 24 m b
63 04 13 f b
63 05 8 f b

HALL, James D.
63 01 36 m b
63 02 30 f b
63 03 12 f m
63 04 12 m b

RECTOR, W. H.
64 01 47 f b
64 01 28 f b
64 01 26 m b
64 01 23 f b
64 01 12 m b
64 01 3 m b

BRASHEAR, Robert
64 01 7 m m
64 01 11 f m
64 01 4 f m

COCHRAN, George L.
64 01 75 f b
64 01 35 f b
64 01 19 f b
64 01 12 d m
64 01 6 f b
64 01 4 f b
64 01 2 f b

FRY, John M.
64 01 18 f b

FRANCIS, Rebecca
64 01 60 f b
64 01 27 f b
64 01 10 m m
64 01 8 m b
64 01 5 f b
64 01 1 m b

MADDUX, Wm. D.
64 01 36 f b
64 01 36 m b
64 01 33 m b
64 01 22 f m
64 01 4 m b
64 01 1 f b

SHACKLETT, Chapman
64 01 60 f b
64 01 30 f b
64 01 22 f b
64 01 14 m b
64 01 8 m b
64 01 4 m b
64 01 2 m b
64 01 1 m b

CHINN, Hugh
64 01 16 f b
64 01 7 f b

HALL, Ducator B.
64 01 23 f b
64 01 18 m b
64 01 15 f b
64 01 11 f b
64 01 3 m b
64 01 1 f b
64 01 8 f b

CLOTHIER, John S.
64 01 23 f b
64 01 2 f b
64 01 9 f m

FLINN, Wm.
64 01 30 f b
64 01 12 f b
64 01 45 m b
64 01 35 m b
64 01 17 m b

ALLEN, Thomas
64 01 27 f b
64 01 18 f b *
* idiotic
64 01 13 f b
64 01 3 f b
64 01 4/12 m b
64 01 35 m b
64 01 27 m b
64 01 18 m m

CELEY, John M.
64 01 29 f b
HANRY, Preston R.
64 01 25 f b
HUNT, Susan
64 01 23 f b
ADAMS, John A.
64 01 50 f b
64 01 24 m b
64 01 18 f m
METCALF, Christopher
64 01 18 f b
64 01 4/12 f b
FLOWERREE, Daniel R.
64 01 42 f b
64 01 20 f b
64 01 22 f b
64 01 38 m b
64 01 14 m b
64 01 7 f b
64 01 11 f m
64 01 1 f b
64 01 3 f b
64 01 2 f b
65 01 8/12 f b
65 01 4/12 m b
SQUIRES, Wm. H.
65 01 14 f b
LAURENCE, Wm.
65 01 65 m b
65 01 44 f b
65 01 18 m b
65 01 1 f b
65 01 10 f b
BRADLEY, Frances
65 01 14 f b
BOWMAN, Leonard
65 01 35 f m
65 01 3 m m
DENNIS, Jessee
65 01 5 m b
FLOWERREE, Wainfield
65 01 35 f b
65 01 15 m b
65 01 13 m b
65 01 10 m b
65 01 5 f b
65 01 3 f b

WELCH, Sylvester
65 01 47 m b
65 01 22 m b
65 01 19 f b
65 01 7 m b
UTTERBACK, Wilford
65 01 40 m b
65 01 25 m b
65 01 74 m b
65 01 35 f b
65 01 14 m b
UTTERBACK, Joseph
65 01 26 f m
65 01 18 f b
65 01 9 m b
65 01 1 m m
HARRELL, Peter
65 01 12 m m
LAWRENCE, Lewis
65 01 48 f b
PAYNE, Elias
65 01 12 m b
BISHOP, James
65 01 34 f b
65 01 31 m b
65 01 9 f b
JEFFRIES, Presly
65 01 42 m b
RUTTER, James
65 01 25 m b
65 01 16 m m
JONES, James F.
65 01 55 m b
65 01 43 f b
65 01 19 m b
65 01 11 m b
65 01 9 f b
65 01 44 f b
65 01 20 m b
65 01 10 m b
65 01 42 m b
65 01 39 f b
65 01 22 m b
65 01 14 f b
65 01 13 m b
65 01 10 m b
65 01 6 m b
65 01 32 f m

65 01 13 f b
65 01 7 m b
65 01 4 m b
65 01 2 f b
65 01 1 m b
65 01 2 f b
65 01 1 m b
65 01 3 f b
65 01 1 f b
65 01 1 f b
65 01 24 f m
65 01 24 f b
65 01 69 m b

WOODARD, Luke
65 01 25 f b
65 01 22 m b
65 01 15 m b
65 01 13 f b
65 01 15 m m
65 01 12 m b
65 01 8 f m
65 01 5 f b
65 01 4 f b
65 01 22 f b
65 01 12 f b
66 01 19 m b
66 01 19 f b
66 01 5 m b
66 01 10/12 m b

SILCOTT, Jacob
66 01 17 f b

ARMISTEAD, Robt. L.
66 01 60 f b
66 01 47 f b
66 01 35 f m
66 01 12 f b
66 01 15 f b
66 01 7 f b
66 01 5 m m
66 01 2 f b
66 01 6/12 m b
66 01 13 m m
66 01 60 m m
66 01 40 m b
66 01 22 m b

SINGLETON, Robt.
66 01 80 m b
66 01 60 m b
66 01 42 m b
66 01 23 m b
66 01 20 m b
66 01 18 m b
66 01 14 m b
66 01 12 m b
66 01 8 m b
66 01 8 m b
66 01 6 m b
66 01 55 f b
66 01 42 f b
66 01 35 f m
66 01 17 f b
66 01 13 f b
66 01 11 f b
66 01 9 f b
66 01 8 f b
66 01 4 f b
66 01 1 f b
66 01 1 f b

HENRY, Edward H.
66 01 60 f b
66 01 45 f b
66 01 26 f b
66 01 20 f m
66 01 12 f b
66 01 3 f m
66 01 3/12 f m
66 01 45 m b
66 01 22 m m
66 01 17 m b
66 01 8 m b
66 01 5 m b
66 01 4 m b

HICKS, Emma
66 01 68 m b
66 01 64 m b
66 01 34 m m
66 01 40 f b
66 01 40 f b
66 01 32 f m
66 01 30 f b
66 01 20 f b
66 01 17 f b
66 01 8 f b
66 01 7 f b
66 01 4 f b
66 01 2 f b

66 01 14 m b
66 01 10 m b
66 01 8 m b
66 01 7 m b
66 01 5 m b
66 01 2 m b
66 01 4 m b
66 01 19 m b

OSBORN, Ann
66 01 27 f b
66 01 12 f b
66 01 4 f b
66 01 4 m b
66 01 2 m b
66 01 3/12 f b

LATHAM, Sarah
67 01 40 m b
67 01 40 f b
67 01 11 m b
67 01 8 m b
67 01 4 f b
67 01 3 m m

CHAPPELIER, Benj'n.
67 01 30 m b
67 01 35 m b
67 01 28 m b
67 01 19 m m
67 01 15 m b
67 01 13 m b
67 01 11 m b
67 01 6 m b
67 01 4 m b
67 01 6 m b
67 01 6 m b
67 01 5 m b
67 01 10/12 m b
67 01 30 f b
67 01 26 f b
67 01 12 f b
67 01 10 f b
67 01 10 f b
67 01 10 f b
67 01 9 f b
67 01 2 f b
67 01 1 f b
67 01 1 f b
67 01 35 m b
67 01 35 m b

KERFOOT, Daniel
67 01 50 m b
67 01 40 m m
67 01 40 m m
67 01 30 m b
67 01 25 m m
67 01 23 m b
67 01 21 m b
67 01 23 m m
67 01 21 m b
67 01 18 m m
67 01 14 m b
67 01 85 m b
67 01 6 m b
67 01 50 m b
67 01 50 f m
67 01 40 f b
67 01 40 f b
67 01 40 f m
67 01 30 f m
67 01 15 f b
67 01 15 f b
67 01 15 f b
67 01 13 f b
67 01 11 f m
67 01 6 f m
67 01 4 m b
67 01 2 m m
67 01 2 f b
67 01 12 f m

BOGGESS, Samuel
67 01 73 f b
67 01 73 f b
67 01 38 m b
67 01 36 f b
67 01 27 f b
67 01 32 m b
67 01 17 m b
67 01 16 f b
67 01 12 m b
67 01 9 f b
67 01 4 f b
67 01 5 f b
67 01 1 f b
67 01 5 m b

FLETCHER, Wm.
67 01 47 m b
67 01 44 m b

67	01	40	m	b
67	01	25	m	b
67	01	18	m	b
67	01	16	m	b
68	01	14	m	b
68	01	4	m	b
68	01	3	m	b
68	01	3	m	b
68	01	2	m	b
68	01	32	f	b
68	01	32	f	b
68	01	16	f	b
68	01	14	f	b
68	01	17	f	b
68	01	13	f	b
68	01	11	f	b
68	01	10	f	b
68	01	8	f	b
68	01	1/12	f	b
68	01	17	m	b

NORRIS, George W.

68	01	25	f	b
68	01	23	f	b

CARTER, Moore F.

68	01	89	m	b
68	01	40	m	b
68	01	25	m	b
68	01	20	m	b
68	01	2	m	b
68	01	22	f	b
68	01	12	f	b
68	01	9	f	b
68	01	3	f	m

EDMONDS, Wm. F.

68	01	76	m	b
68	01	75	m	b
68	01	75	f	b
68	01	72	f	b
68	01	56	m	b
68	01	38	f	b
68	01	28	f	b
68	01	29	m	b
68	01	21	f	b
68	01	13	f	b
68	01	11	m	b
68	01	9	f	b
68	01	7	f	b
68	01	5	m	b
68	01	2	m	b
68	01	10	m	b
68	01	5	m	b
68	01	6	f	b

CARTER, Thomas O.

68	01	68	m	b
68	01	67	f	m
68	01	33	f	b
68	01	16	f	m
68	01	11	m	b
68	01	28	m	b
68	01	7	m	b
68	01	6	f	b
68	01	4	m	b

CARTER, Judith

68	01	80	f	b
68	01	66	f	b
68	01	42	f	m
68	01	35	f	b
68	01	26	f	m
68	01	22	f	m
68	01	20	f	b
68	01	13	f	b
68	01	11	f	b
68	01	7	f	b
68	01	5	f	m
68	01	5	f	m
68	01	4	f	b
68	01	1	f	b
68	01	6/12	f	m
68	01	4	f	m
68	01	?	f	m
68	01	21	m	m
68	01	13	m	m
68	01	12	m	b
68	01	9	m	m
68	01	5	m	b
68	01	3	m	b
68	01	2	m	b
68	01	2	m	m
68	01	40	m	b
69	01	40	m	b
69	01	25	m	b
69	01	25	m	b
69	01	15	m	b
69	01	50	f	b
69	01	40	f	b
69	01	10	m	b

69 01 5 m b
THOMAS, Wm.
69 01 58 f m
PENQUITE, Kissiah
69 01 26 f b
69 01 9 m b
69 01 5 m b
69 01 3 m b
69 01 2 m b
69 01 2/12 m b
FLETCHER, Alpheus
69 01 54 f b
69 01 30 m b
69 01 22 m b
69 01 21 m b
LUFFBOROUGH, Nathan
69 01 38 m b
69 01 33 m b
69 01 17 m b
69 01 13 m b
69 01 11 m b
69 01 7 m b
69 01 4 m b
69 01 3 m m
69 01 1 m b
69 01 1 m b
69 01 55 f b
69 01 30 f b
69 01 30 f b
69 01 27 f m
69 01 21 f b
69 01 4 f b
69 01 2 f b
69 01 37 f b
69 01 6 f m
69 01 4 f b
ROBINSON, John G.
69 01 28 m b
69 01 27 f b
69 01 11 f b
69 01 8 f b
69 01 6 f b
69 01 4 m b
69 01 2 f b
69 01 25 m b
CARR, Caldwell
69 01 65 f b
69 01 65 f b
69 01 48 f b
69 01 44 m b
69 01 27 m b
69 01 22 m m
69 01 4 m b
69 01 2 m b
69 01 34 f m
69 01 19 f m
YEARBY, Wm. G.
69 01 37 m b
69 01 32 f b
69 01 20 f b
69 01 12 m b
69 01 12 f b
69 01 6 m b
69 01 1/12 f b
STEPHENSON, Wm. A.
69 01 40 f b
69 01 47 f m
69 01 56 f m
69 01 21 f m
69 01 17 f b
69 01 16 m m
69 01 33 m b
69 01 9 f m
69 01 6 f m
69 01 4 f m
69 01 9/12 f m
69 01 1 m m
BROWN, George M.
69 01 50 f b
69 01 20 f m
69 01 20 m m
69 01 10 f b
70 01 12 f m
70 01 10 m m
70 01 6 f b
70 01 3 f b
WARD, Joel
70 01 8 f b
PIERCE, Charity
70 01 10 f b
SCOTT, Moses
70 01 9 f m
LUNCEFORD, Harison
70 01 80 f b
70 01 22 m b
70 01 19 f b

70 01 16 m b
70 01 12 f b
BALL, Franklin
70 01 12 m b
PIERCE, Amos
70 01 14 m b
70 01 15 m b
70 01 17 f b
70 01 22 m b
70 01 42 m b
LAWRENCE, Patia
70 01 20 f b
70 01 10 f b
WHITE, Elizabeth
70 01 9 f b
HARDY, Wm.
70 01 35 f b
70 01 7 m b
70 01 3 m b
HUTCHERSON, Lemuel
70 01 35 m b
70 01 35 m b
70 01 25 f b
70 01 25 f m
70 01 16 m b
70 01 10 f b
70 01 7 m b
70 01 6 f b
70 01 6 f m
70 01 4 m b
70 01 3 f m
70 01 2 m m
70 01 1 f b
DIXON, Henry T.
70 01 16 f m
70 01 14 f m
70 01 20 f b
70 01 45 f b
DODGE, Henry W.
70 01 80 m b
70 01 50 f b
70 01 15 f b
McKINSTER, Haurace
70 01 25 m m
70 01 19 f m
70 01 16 f b
JOLLY, Bushrod
70 01 19 m b
70 01 20 m b
70 01 40 f b
70 01 20 f b
70 01 18 f b
70 01 10 f b
70 01 1 f b
70 01 30 f b
70 01 1 m b
70 01 50 m b
COLSTON, Raghle
70 01 27 f b
70 01 12 f b
70 01 10 f b
70 01 1 m b
DURAL, James S. H.
70 01 26 f b
70 01 14 f m
70 01 20 m m
EDMONDS, John R.
70 01 40 f m
70 01 19 f m
70 01 13 f b
70 01 2 f m
70 01 2/12 m m
TAYLOR, Agnes
70 01 32 m m
70 01 27 f b
70 01 5 f b
70 01 5 f b
BRENT, Willis
70 01 31 f b
70 01 10 m b
70 01 5 f b
70 01 4/12 m b
FLEMING, John
70 01 11 m b
FOLK, John
70 01 21 f b
70 01 4/12 m m
WALKER, James W.
71 01 40 m b
HOLMS, Franklin T.
71 01 20 f b
REID, Stephen
71 01 14 f b
SMITH, Ann
71 01 40 m m
71 01 35 f b

71 01 27 f b
71 01 15 m b
71 01 15 m b
71 01 12 f b
71 01 14 f b
71 01 8 m b
71 01 7 m b
71 01 5 m b
71 01 3 m b
71 01 4 f b
71 01 3 f b
71 01 8/12 f b
71 01 40 m b

BROWN, George
71 01 55 m b
71 01 8 f b
71 01 18 m b
71 01 26 m b
71 01 19 m b
71 01 25 m b
71 01 60 m b
71 01 10 m b
71 01 7 f b
71 01 5 m b
71 01 4 m b
71 01 4 f b
71 01 2 f b
71 01 12 f b
71 01 40 f b

FLEMING, Sarah L.
71 01 9 f b

WHITE, Wesly
71 01 8 m b

WIDOWS, Rosa
71 01 12 f b

HERIFORD, Margaret
71 01 27 m m
71 01 43 f m
71 01 18 f b
71 01 16 f b
71 01 10 m m
71 01 9 f b
71 01 10/12 f b
71 01 5/12 f b

BYRNE, James
71 01 12 f b

SPAULDING, George S.
71 01 16 f b

CALVERT, George
71 01 60 f b
71 01 49 m m
71 01 40 f b
71 01 58 f b
71 01 13 m m
71 01 11 m m
71 01 9 m m

HARPER, Joel. H.
71 01 52 m b
71 01 14 m m
71 01 7 m b
71 01 50 f b
71 01 14 f b
71 01 20 f b

CARTER, Eliza F.
71 01 45 m b
71 01 45 m b
71 01 15 f m
71 01 14 m b
71 01 5 m b
71 01 3 m b
71 01 8/12 f m

CARTER, Robert
71 01 60 m b
71 01 55 f b
71 01 33 m b
71 01 32 m b
71 01 30 m b
71 01 25 m b
71 01 28 m b
71 01 24 m b
71 01 23 f b
71 01 16 f b
71 01 10 f m
71 01 9 f m
71 01 6 m m
72 01 4 m m
72 01 4 f b
72 01 3/12 m b

WHITING, G. W. C.
72 01 40 f b
72 01 22 f m
72 01 17 f b
72 01 45 f b
72 01 33 m b
72 01 30 m b
72 01 19 m m

72	01	18	m	m
72	01	11	m	b
72	01	25	m	b
72	01	30	m	b
72	01	18	m	b
72	01	3	f	m
72	01	10/12	m	m
72	01	50	m	m
BOWIE, Nimrod S.				
72	01	11	f	b
DEBUTTS, Richard				
72	01	70	f	b
72	01	45	m	b
72	01	35	m	b
72	01	28	f	b
72	01	18	f	b
72	01	15	m	b
72	01	11	m	b
72	01	11	f	b
72	01	9	f	b
72	01	6	f	b
72	01	6	f	b
72	01	3	f	b
72	01	5	m	b
72	01	1	m	b
72	01	7/12	m	b
GLASCOCK, Thomas				
72	01	50	m	b
72	01	45	f	b
72	01	23	m	b
72	01	22	m	b
72	01	22	f	b
72	01	21	f	b
72	01	14	m	b
72	01	13	f	b
72	01	7	f	b
72	01	5	m	b
72	01	5	m	b
72	01	5	m	b
72	01	4	m	b
72	01	3	m	b
72	01	3	m	b
72	01	2	m	b
72	01	2	f	b
72	01	1	m	b
GLASCOCK, Aquilla				
72	01	30	f	b
72	01	10	m	b
72	01	8	f	b
72	01	6	f	b
72	01	4	m	b
72	01	2	m	b
72	01	7	f	b
72	01	6	f	b
GLASCOCK, George				
72	01	52	m	b
72	01	47	m	b
72	01	33	m	b
72	01	32	m	b
72	01	20	m	m
72	01	17	m	b
72	01	5	m	b
72	01	44	f	b
72	01	17	f	b
72	01	8	f	b
72	01	5	f	b
72	01	1	f	m
72	01	1/12	f	b
72	01	1/12	m	m
72	01	1/12	m	m
72	01	18	m	b
RECTOR, Benj.				
72	01	18	f	m
72	01	78	f	b
72	01	78	m	b *
		* blind		
72	01	54	m	b
GLASCOCK, Robt. T.				
73	01	32	f	b
73	01	8	f	b
73	01	5	f	b
73	01	1	m	b
BALTHROPE, John H.				
73	01	35	f	b
73	01	4	f	m
73	01	2	m	b
73	01	4/12	f	m
COCKE, Wm.				
73	01	25	f	b
73	01	25	m	b
73	01	21	m	b
73	01	16	f	b
73	01	16	f	b
73	01	15	f	m
73	01	10	m	b
73	01	10	f	m

73 01 6 m b
73 01 3 f b
73 01 1 f b

STROTHER, James S.
73 01 45 f b
73 01 1 m b

PURSELL, A. S.
73 01 35 m b
73 01 9 m b
73 01 5 f b
73 01 2 f b

DUNCAN, Elsy
73 01 85 m b
73 01 65 f b
73 01 10 m b

RECTOR, John
73 01 25 f m
73 01 33 f b
73 01 3 f m
73 01 5 f b
73 01 2 f b
73 01 5/12 f b

RECTOR, Henry
73 01 17 f b
73 01 21 f b

FROBEL, Bushrod
73 01 32 f b
73 01 20 m m
73 01 8 m b
73 01 5 f m
73 01 5 m b

STEPHENSON, Hiram
73 01 31 f b
73 01 25 m b

COCKE, Kemp F.
73 01 31 m b
73 01 20 f b
73 01 11 f m
73 01 5 m b
73 01 3/12 m m
73 01 3/12 f m

WEBSTER, Catharine
73 01 75 f b

VANHORN, Burr W.
73 01 9 f b

COMPTON, Lawson
73 01 14 f b
73 01 7 f b

WOLFE, John
73 01 25 f b
73 01 9 m b
73 01 7 m b
73 01 5 f b

PRIEST, James
73 01 43 m b
73 01 30 f b
73 01 24 f b
73 01 22 m b
73 01 21 m b
73 01 22 f b
73 01 15 m b
73 01 12 f b
73 01 8 m b
73 01 7 f b
73 01 7 f b
73 01 5 f m
73 01 4 m b
73 01 4 m b
73 01 3 m b
73 01 3 m b
73 01 1 m b
73 01 1 m b
73 01 7/12 m b

DOWELL, Wm. F.
73 01 68 m m
73 01 75 f b
73 01 54 m b
73 01 25 m b
74 01 30 f b
74 01 22 f b
74 01 17 m b
74 01 15 f b
74 01 8 f b
74 01 3 f b
74 01 2 m b

SILCOTT, James H.
74 01 14 f b

THOMPSON, James
74 01 75 m b
74 01 17 m b
74 01 30 f b
74 01 10 m b
74 01 8 m b

FOSTER, James W.
74 01 76 m b
74 01 50 m b

74	01	41	m	b
74	01	40	m	b
74	01	26	m	b
74	01	17	m	b
74	01	11	m	b
74	01	7	m	b
74	01	5	m	b
74	01	4	m	b
74	01	40	f	b
74	01	38	f	b
74	01	28	f	b
74	01	13	f	b
74	01	11	f	b
74	01	4	f	b
74	01	2	m	b

CHAPMAN, Alexander

74	01	22	m	b
74	01	27	m	b
74	01	6	m	b
74	01	15	m	b
74	01	6	m	b
74	01	5	m	b
74	01	4	m	b
74	01	3	m	b
74	01	3	m	b
74	01	30	f	b
74	01	25	f	b
74	01	25	f	b
74	01	6	f	b
74	01	6	f	b
74	01	1	f	b
74	01	2/12	f	b

SULLIVAN, Luthur O.

74	01	40	m	b
74	01	24	m	b
74	01	22	f	b
74	01	6/12	f	b

MURRAY, James E.

74	01	60	f	b
74	01	30	f	b
74	01	25	f	b
74	01	26	f	b
74	01	23	f	m
74	01	18	f	b
74	01	12	f	b
74	01	8	f	m
74	01	8	f	b
74	01	8	f	b
74	01	5	f	b
74	01	3	f	b
74	01	1	f	b
74	01	46	m	b
74	01	25	m	b
74	01	20	m	b
74	01	13	m	b
74	01	12	m	b
74	01	10	m	m
74	01	6	m	b
74	01	5	m	b
74	01	4	m	b
74	01	3	m	b

SUMMERS, George W.

74	01	30	f	b
74	01	21	m	b
74	01	15	m	b
74	01	13	m	b
74	01	10	m	m
74	01	9	m	b
74	01	4	f	b

SUMMERS, Ludwell

75	01	28	f	b
75	01	7	m	b
75	01	5	f	b
75	01	4	m	b

TAYLOR, Wm. P.

75	01	95	f	b
75	01	38	m	m
75	01	17	m	b
75	01	14	f	b
75	01	12	m	m
75	01	8	f	b

FISHBACK, Nancy

75	01	60	m	b
75	01	30	m	b
75	01	16	m	b
75	01	15	m	b
75	01	13	m	b
75	01	12	m	b
75	01	50	f	b
75	01	49	f	b
75	01	30	f	m
75	01	22	f	b
75	01	5	f	b
75	01	30	f	b
75	01	7	f	b
75	01	5	f	b

75 01 6 f m
75 01 16 f m
75 01 2 f b
75 01 1/12 f b

BYRNE, Wm.

75 01 45 m m
75 01 47 m b
75 01 30 m b
75 01 30 m m
75 01 25 m b
75 01 22 m b
75 01 18 m b
75 01 28 m m
75 01 22 m b
75 01 15 m m
75 01 17 m m
75 01 26 m b
75 01 48 f b
75 01 34 f m
75 01 36 f m
75 01 25 f m
75 01 20 f b
75 01 15 f b
75 01 17 f m
75 01 10 f b
75 01 25 f b
75 01 14 m m
75 01 8 m b
75 01 7 f b
75 01 6 f b
75 01 5 f b
75 01 4 f b
75 01 1 m b
75 01 8 m m
75 01 6 m b
75 01 4 m b
75 01 2 m b
75 01 3 m b
75 01 1 m b
75 01 3/12 f m
75 01 2 m b
75 01 21 m m

UTTERBACK, Briant

75 01 50 f b
75 01 30 f b
75 01 25 m b
75 01 13 m b

FOSTER, Priscilla

75 01 77 m b
75 01 50 f b
75 01 50 m b
75 01 43 m b
75 01 18 m b
75 01 15 m b
75 01 23 f b
75 01 5 m b
75 01 3 f b
75 01 2 f b
75 01 7/12 f b
75 01 ?/12 m b
76 01 1? f b
76 01 10 f b
76 01 5 m b

GRIFFITH, John

76 01 30 m b

GRIFFITH, Elizabeth

76 01 65 f b
76 01 45 m b
76 01 32 f b
76 01 23 m b
76 01 21 m b
76 01 12 m b
76 01 10 f b
76 01 4 f b

TURNER, Edward C.

76 01 28 f m
76 01 21 f b
76 01 60 f b
76 01 60 m b
76 01 4 f m
76 01 35 m b
76 01 26 m b
76 01 38 f b

FINCH, Wm. H.

76 01 27 m b
76 01 25 m b

SMITH, James W.

76 01 30 f b
76 01 3 f b
76 01 1/12 m b

HOWDERSHELL, Jacob

76 01 43 f b
76 01 7 m b
76 01 2 f b

CLARKE, Thomas W.

76 01 10 f b

SMITH, Alexander M.
76 01 58 m b
76 01 30 m b
76 01 28 m b
76 01 16 m b
76 01 13 m b
76 01 18 f b
76 01 13 f b
76 01 14 f b
76 01 4 f b
ELGIN, John T.
76 01 7 m b
BELT, Greenberry
76 01 15 f b
MATHEWS, Squire E.
76 01 55 f b
76 01 24 m b
76 01 17 f b
76 01 15 f b
76 01 5 m m
76 01 3 m b
76 01 1 f b
HATHAWAY, Henry L.
76 01 48 f b
76 01 38 f b
76 01 25 m b
76 01 22 f b
76 01 17 m b
76 01 10 m b
76 01 6 m b
76 01 5 f b
GLASCOCK, Wm. R.
76 01 42 m b
76 01 26 m b
76 01 15 m b
76 01 9 m b
76 01 7 m b
76 01 4 f b
76 01 40 f b
DEER, George W.
76 01 21 f b
76 01 12 f b
76 01 4 f m
76 01 7/12 m b
76 01 35 m b
76 01 34 m b
76 01 44 m b
76 01 13 m b
SULLIVAN, John
76 01 60 f b
76 01 60 f b
76 01 42 f m
76 01 45 m m
76 01 45 m b
76 01 22 m m
76 01 16 m m
76 01 15 m m
76 01 15 m b
77 01 13 m m
77 01 11 m m
77 01 10 m m
77 01 10 m b
77 01 9 m b
77 01 9 m m
77 01 13 f b
77 01 10 f b
77 01 9 f b
77 01 2 m b
CRANE, Bailey
77 01 45 m b
77 01 35 m b
77 01 21 m b
77 01 19 m b
77 01 22 f b
77 01 15 m b
77 01 12 m b
77 01 10 m b
77 01 8 m b
77 01 1 f b
PORTER, Maurace
77 01 6 f b
COCHRAN, John
77 01 40 m b
77 01 35 m b
77 01 35 f b
77 01 15 f b
THRIFT, Francis E.
77 01 39 m b
77 01 35 f b
77 01 35 f m
77 01 19 m b
77 01 10 f b
77 01 7 f b
77 01 6 f b
77 01 5 m m
77 01 3 f b

77 01 1 f m
77 01 3/12 m m
77 01 3/12 m m
77 01 16 m b

RATCLIFF, Quinton
77 01 25 f b
77 01 21 m b
77 01 16 f b
77 01 6 f b
77 01 3 f b
77 01 1 f b

SULLIVAN, Mary
77 01 105 m b
77 01 65 f m
77 01 65 f b
77 01 45 m b
77 01 38 f b
77 01 25 m b
77 01 36 m m
77 01 21 m b
77 01 19 m m
77 01 20 f m
77 01 10? m b
77 01 21 m b
77 01 14 f b
77 01 10 f b
77 01 7 f b
77 01 6 m b
77 01 4 m b
77 01 1 m b
77 01 5 m b
77 01 3 f b
77 01 6/12 f b

LUNCEFORD, Wormley
77 01 37 f b
77 01 2/12 f b

JOHNSON, Amos
77 01 25 f b

BIRCH, Thomas
77 01 35 m b
77 01 17 f b
77 01 9 m b

SIMPSON, Charles
77 01 60 m b
77 01 24 f b
77 01 20 m b
77 01 12 f b
77 01 2 f b
77 01 1/12 m b

CRAIG, Samuel
77 01 25 f b
77 01 25 m b
77 01 4 m b
78 01 3 f b
78 01 1 f b

LOGAN, John
78 01 15 m m *
* deaf

TRIPLETT, Richard
78 01 60 m b
78 01 45 m b
78 01 40 m m
78 01 30 m b
78 01 20 m b
78 01 45 f b
78 01 15 f b
78 01 14 m b
78 01 13 m b
78 01 11 m b
78 01 10 m b
78 01 9 m b
78 01 8 f b
78 01 7 f b
78 01 2 m b

RECTOR, Spencer
78 01 40 f b
78 01 37 m b
78 01 30 m b
78 01 16 m b
78 01 15 m b
78 01 13 m b
78 01 10 m b
78 01 10 m b
78 01 14 f b
78 01 12 f b
78 01 7 f b
78 01 8 f b

HITIFER, John
78 01 12 m b

NOLAND, Lloyd
78 01 54 m b
78 01 40 m b
78 01 33 m b
78 01 33 m b
78 01 28 m m
78 01 50 m b

78 01 40 m b
78 01 30 f b
78 01 27 f b
78 01 25 f b
78 01 11 m b
78 01 9 m b
78 01 6 m b
78 01 3 m b
78 01 1 m b
78 01 8 f b
78 01 7 f b *
* idiotic
78 01 6 f b
78 01 5 f b
78 01 4 f b
78 01 3 f b
78 01 6 m b
78 01 4 m b
78 01 10 f b

CRANE, James
78 01 78 m b
78 01 72 f b
78 01 64 f b
78 01 39 m b
78 01 37 m b
78 01 29 f b
78 01 28 m b *
* fugitive
78 01 26 f b
78 01 22 m b
78 01 14 f b
78 01 5 f b
78 01 3 f b
78 01 1/12 m b
78 01 1/12 f b

WATERS, Jonathan
78 01 40 m b
78 01 25 f b
78 01 14 m b
78 01 10 f b
78 01 9 m b
78 01 6 m b
78 01 4 m b
78 01 6/12 m b
78 01 18 f b

MIDDLETON, Thomas
78 01 30 f b
78 01 20 m b
79 01 17 f b
79 01 14 m b
79 01 11 m b
79 01 7 f b
79 01 6 m b
79 01 4 f b
79 01 2 f b
79 01 3/12 m b

PATTERSON, John W.
79 01 40 f b
79 01 33 f m
79 01 30 f b
79 01 22 m m
79 01 20 m b
79 01 18 m m
79 01 17 m b
79 01 14 m m
79 01 14 m b
79 01 14 m b
79 01 12 m b
79 01 12 f b
79 01 11 f b
79 01 8 f b
79 01 8 f b
79 01 6 f b
79 01 5 m b
79 01 4 f b
79 01 2 f b
79 01 8 m b
79 01 1 f b
79 01 80 f b *
* blind

LUNCEFORD, Baldwin
79 01 20 m b
79 01 16 f b
79 01 14 f b
79 01 12 f b
79 01 12 m b
79 01 8 f b
79 01 4 m b
79 01 2 m b

PINKETT, James S.
79 01 56 m b
79 01 56 m b
79 01 45 m b
79 01 22 m b
79 01 16 m b
79 01 16 m b

79 01 14 m b
79 01 8 m b
79 01 6 m b
79 01 49 f b
79 01 45 f b
79 01 21 f b
79 01 7 f b

GRAYHAM, Hugh S.
79 01 34 f b
79 01 12 f b

MARTIN, Thomas
79 01 32 m b
79 01 25 f b
79 01 62 m b
79 01 27 m b
79 01 10 f b
79 01 2 m b

VIOLETT, Sarah
79 01 30 f b
79 01 4 f b
79 01 2 m b
79 01 36 m b

DAVIS, Travis
79 01 37 m b
79 01 34 f b
79 01 12 f b
79 01 10 m b
79 01 6 f b
79 01 4 f b
79 01 2 m b
79 01 2 m b
79 01 1 m b
79 01 13 m b

MOORE, Henry
79 01 11 f m

ANDERSON, Harison
79 01 48 f b
79 01 25 m b
79 01 14 m m
79 01 ?/12 f b
79 01 ? m b
79 01 3? m b

MITCHELL, Benj'n E.
80 01 9 m b

MITCHELL, James
80 01 16 f b

LYNN, John
80 01 66 m b
80 01 48 f m

MURRAY, Alfred
80 01 62 m b
80 01 53 f b
80 01 35 m b
80 01 27 f b
80 01 25 m b
80 01 18 m b
80 01 17 m b
80 01 10 f b
80 01 1 f b

LAWSON, James W.
80 01 21 m b
80 01 16 f b
80 01 5 f b

PULLER, Samuel
80 01 26 m b
80 01 12 m b
80 01 30 f b
80 01 6 f b
80 01 4 f b
80 01 1 f b

PICKETT, John
80 01 16 f b
80 01 18 f b

SAUNDERS, Larken N.
80 01 15 f b
80 01 9 m b
80 01 60 f b

ROBINSON, Samuel T.
80 01 10 m b

SISK, James
80 01 65 f b
80 01 10 m b

GLASCOCK, Burr
80 01 13 f b

CROUCH, Wm.
80 01 65 f b

DENT, Wm. F.
80 01 25 m b
80 01 17 f b
80 01 17 m b

SEATON, Hiriam K.
80 01 16 f b
80 01 10 f b
80 01 13 m b
80 01 18 m b

RECTOR, Margaret

80 01 55 f b
80 01 60 m b
80 01 60 m b

BALL, Peyton
80 01 24 m b
80 01 17 m b

GLASCOCK, Minor
80 01 11 f b

SMITH, Henry
80 01 45 m m
80 01 35 f b
80 01 29 m b
80 01 18 f b
80 01 17 m b
80 01 14 f b
80 01 10 m b
80 01 8 f b
80 01 7 f b
80 01 6 m b
80 01 4 m b
80 01 2 m b

DAWSON, George
80 01 55 f b

BRENT, Fayette
80 01 48 m b
80 01 50 m b
80 01 25 f b
80 01 13 f b

COCKE, Wellington
80 01 37 m b
80 01 37 f b
80 01 30 m b
80 01 30 f b
80 01 16 m b
80 01 12 f b
80 01 11 f b
80 01 10 m b
80 01 8 m b
80 01 8 m b
80 01 7 m b
80 01 7 f b
80 01 6 m b
80 01 5 m b
80 01 4 f b
80 01 3 m b

BAILEY, Sampson P.
80 01 50 f m
80 01 40 m m
81 01 35 m b
81 01 17 m b
81 01 16 m b
81 01 16 f b
81 01 11 m b
81 01 12 f m

FOSTER, Thomas R.
81 01 47 m b
81 01 46 f b
81 01 32 f b
81 01 22 m b
81 01 20 f m
81 01 18 f b
81 01 15 m b
81 01 8 m b
81 01 6 m b
81 01 4 m b
81 01 3 m b
81 01 2 m b
81 01 4/12 m b
81 01 1 m b

CARTER, Henry
81 01 35 f b
81 01 2/12 f b

BRENT, Hugh
81 01 66 m b
81 01 42 m m
81 01 40 f b
81 01 23 m b
81 01 18 f b

GIBSON, Jessee
81 01 15 f b

FLOWERREE, Contee
81 01 60 m b
81 01 55 f b
81 01 50 f b
81 01 50 m b *
* idiotic
81 01 30 m b
81 01 20 m b
81 01 17 f b
81 01 11 m b

LAWLER, Wm.
81 01 37 m b
81 01 28 m b
81 01 25 m b
81 01 25 f b
81 01 70 f b

81 01 55 f b
81 01 27 m b
81 01 25 m b
81 01 22 m b
81 01 18 m b
81 01 14 m b
81 01 11 f b
81 01 5 m b
81 01 2 m b
81 01 8 f b
81 01 5 m b
81 01 3 f b
81 01 2/12 f b

DODD, Mason B.
81 01 12 m b

HOWDERSHELL, John
81 01 37 f m
81 01 18 f m
81 01 8 f m
81 01 16 m m

LUNCEFORD, James
81 01 35 m b
81 01 18 f b

OWENS, Joshua
81 01 40 f b
81 01 6 m b
81 01 4 f b
81 01 3 f m
81 01 3/12 m b

MARTIN, Wm. A.
81 01 30 f b
81 01 28 m b
81 01 13 m b

FOLEY, Enoch
81 01 55 f b
81 01 9 m b
81 01 7 f b
81 01 12 f b

OWENS, Elizabeth
81 01 60 m b
81 01 45 m b
81 01 35 f b
81 01 32 f b
81 01 14 f b
81 01 12 f b
81 01 11 m b
82 01 9 f b
82 01 7 m b
82 01 5 f b
82 01 5 f b
82 01 3 m b
82 01 2 f b
82 01 2 f b
82 01 3/12 f b
82 01 2/12 m b
82 01 19 m b

OWENS, Thomas F.
82 01 50 f m
82 01 11 m b
82 01 8 f m

COMBS, Burr
82 01 70 f b
82 01 26 m b
82 01 25 f b
82 01 11 f b
82 01 7 m m
82 01 5 m b
82 01 2 m m

TAVENER, Samuel
82 01 20 f b
82 01 4/12 f b

ROSE, Wm.
82 01 15 m b

PULLER, James
82 01 10 f b

SMITH, Roley
82 01 9 m b

TURNER, Henry H.
82 01 70 f b
82 01 21 f b
82 01 22 m b
82 01 12 m b
82 01 10 m b
82 01 7 f b
82 01 5 m b
82 01 3 f b
82 01 2 m b
82 01 1 f b

FINCH, James
82 01 20 f b

LUNCEFORD, Benjamine
82 01 26 f b
82 01 25 f b
82 01 1 f b

CREEL, Sirepta
82 01 15 f b

GRIFFITH, Iven
82 01 40 f b
82 01 38 m b
82 01 22 f b
82 01 13 f b
82 01 7 m b
KIRKPATRICK, Wm.
82 01 15 m b
DOWNS, James
82 01 85 f b
82 01 17 m b
HENDERSON, Thomas
82 01 28 m b
82 01 55 m m
82 01 42 m b
82 01 25 m b
82 01 25 f b
82 01 12 f b
82 01 5 m b
82 01 3 m b
82 01 1 f b
SULLIVAN, Willis
82 01 19 m b
82 01 30 f m
82 01 10 m b
82 01 7 m b
82 01 13 f b
82 01 4 f b
82 01 2 m b
82 01 3/12 m b
SWARTZ, Catharine
82 01 11 m b
STOVER, Charles
82 01 35 f b
NORRIS, Thomas
82 01 31 f b
82 01 34 m m
82 01 9 m b
82 01 7 m m
82 01 6 m m
82 01 5 m m
82 01 2 m m
82 01 30 f b
82 01 12 f b
82 01 8 f m
82 01 6 m m
82 01 4 f b
82 01 20 m b
83 01 65 m b
83 01 60 f b
83 01 55 f b
83 01 10 f m
83 01 6 f m
83 01 80 f b
SMARR, Charles
83 01 40 f b
83 01 35 f b
83 01 26 m b
83 01 21 m b
83 01 17 m b
83 01 20 f b
83 01 16 f b
83 01 12 f b
83 01 12 m b
83 01 10 m b
83 01 8 m b
83 01 7 m b
83 01 5 m b
83 01 5 m b
83 01 5 m b
83 01 10 f b
83 01 8 f b
83 01 4 m b
83 01 4 m b
83 01 3 m b
83 01 2 m b
83 01 2 m b
83 01 1 m b
83 01 7/12 f b
HALLEY, Samuel H.
83 01 24 f b
83 01 19 m m
83 01 5 f m
83 01 2 m m
GLASCOCK, Mary
83 01 56 f b
83 01 11 m b
83 01 14 f b
SEATON, James P.
83 01 60 f b
83 01 20 m b
83 01 15 m b
83 01 11 f b
83 01 60 m b
DUNCAN, Charles
83 01 28 m b

83 01 25 m b
83 01 23 m b
83 01 20 m b
83 01 18 m b
83 01 14 m b
83 01 7 m b
83 01 45 f b
83 01 30 f b
83 01 20 f b
83 01 18 f b
83 01 12 f b
83 01 5 f b
83 01 4 f b
83 01 4 f b
83 01 3 f b

MOFFETT, Andrew F.
83 01 22 f b
83 01 2 m m
83 01 1 m m

PEYTON, Robert E.
83 01 72 m b
83 01 50 f b
83 01 30 m b
83 01 24 f b
83 01 20 m b
83 01 66 f b
83 01 7 f b
83 01 3 m m
83 01 1 m m
83 01 30 f m
83 01 25 m m
83 01 15 f b
83 01 6 f m
83 01 5 f m
83 01 2 m m
83 01 7/12 m m
83 01 13 f b
83 01 40 m m
83 01 75 f b
84 01 5 m b

HATHAWAY, James H.
84 01 70 m b
84 01 65 f b
84 01 35 m b
84 01 25 m b
84 01 26 m b
84 01 21 m b
84 01 32 f b
84 01 32 f b
84 01 17 f b
84 01 14 m b
84 01 11 f b
84 01 7 f b
84 01 8 f b
84 01 3 m b
84 01 6/12 f b
84 01 24 m b

CARTER, Wm. F.
84 01 50 f b
84 01 13 f b
84 01 10 m b

LAKE, Isaac
84 01 44 m b
84 01 36 m m
84 01 16 m b
84 01 12 m b
84 01 9 m m
84 01 7 m m
84 01 10 m m
84 01 6 m m
84 01 32 f b
84 01 28 f b
84 01 16 f m
84 01 10 f b
84 01 6 f m
84 01 2 f m

KINCHELOE, Brandt
84 01 22 f b
84 01 22 m b
84 01 21 m b

BALTHROPE, Jeremiah W.
84 01 60 m b
84 01 23 f b
84 01 1? f b
84 01 8 f b

WOLFE, Andrew Sen.
84 01 50 f b
84 01 20 m m

SAMPSELL, Andrew J.
84 01 45 m b
84 01 45 f b
84 01 25 m b
84 01 20 m b
84 01 16 f b
84 01 2 f b

MURRAY, John

84 01 26 m b
84 01 22 f b
84 01 19? f b
84 01 16 m b
84 01 12 m b
84 01 7 m b
84 01 2 m b

MAXWELL, Thomas
84 01 20 f b
84 01 1 f m

BERRYMAN, Ottaway
84 01 30 m b
84 01 26 m m
84 01 30 f m
84 01 20 f b
84 01 14 f b
84 01 10 m b
84 01 7 m m
84 01 3 m b
84 01 1 f b

CHAMBLIN, Stephen
84 01 11 m b

PIERCE, Lafayette
84 01 19 m b
84 01 48 f b

REID, Alfred Jun.
84 01 44 f b
84 01 4 f b
84 01 25 f b
84 01 2 f b
84 01 1 f b
84 01 24 m b

RECTOR, James H.
84 01 62 f b
84 01 23 f b
84 01 9 f m
84 01 7 f m
85 01 4 m b
85 01 25 f b
85 01 18 f b
85 01 40 m b

COOKE, John G.
85 01 21 f m
85 01 10 f b
85 01 8/12 m m

SIMPSON, John
85 01 15 f b

FLOWERREE, Daniel A.
85 01 75 f b
85 01 45 f b
85 01 25 f b
85 01 30 m b
85 01 19 m b
85 01 14 m b
85 01 10 f m
85 01 4 f m
85 01 2 f m

TRIPLETT, Levin
85 01 25 f b
85 01 14 f b
85 01 6 f m
85 01 3 m m
85 01 6/12 m m

GRACE, Christena
85 01 42 f b
85 01 8 f b
85 01 1 m b

GLASCOCK, Wm.
85 01 64 f m
85 01 27 f m
85 01 9 f m
85 01 7 f m
85 01 5 m m
85 01 3 m m
85 01 1 f m
85 01 22 f b
85 01 3 f m
85 01 1 f b
85 01 20 f b
85 01 3 f b
85 01 1/12 f b
85 01 4 m b
85 01 2 m b
85 01 16 f m
85 01 13 f b
85 01 65 m b
85 01 56 m b
85 01 40 m b
85 01 40 m b
85 01 38 m b
85 01 26 m b
85 01 23 m b
85 01 15 m b
85 01 9 m b

GLASCOCK, John
85 01 55 m b

85 01 50 f b
85 01 36 f b
85 01 26 m b
85 01 14 m b
85 01 13 m b
85 01 12 m b
85 01 7 m b
85 01 5 f b
85 01 5 f b
85 01 10 f b
85 01 7 m b
85 01 5 m b
85 01 3 f b
85 01 14 m b
85 01 1 m b

RECTOR, Margaret
85 01 55 f b
85 01 45 m b
85 01 25 f b
85 01 16 m b
85 01 7 f b

HOGUE, Joshua
85 01 38 f b
85 01 27 f b
85 01 25 m b
85 01 21 f b
85 01 17 f b
85 01 14 m b
85 01 12 m b
85 01 10 f b
86 01 7 m b
86 01 6 f b
86 01 4 f b
86 01 2 f b

DENHAM, David
86 01 67 f b
86 01 7 m b
86 01 6 m b
86 01 4 f m

RECTOR, Alfred
86 01 60 f b
86 01 50 f b
86 01 50 f b
86 01 40 f b
86 01 20 f b
86 01 12 f b
86 01 4 f b
86 01 30 m b
86 01 30 m b
86 01 30 m m
86 01 28 m b
86 01 25 m b
86 01 17 m b *
* idiotic
86 01 14 m b
86 01 10 m b
86 01 8 m b
86 01 7 m b
86 01 2 m b
86 01 45 m b *
* blind

BAKER, Alexander
86 01 40 m b
86 01 35 m b
86 01 35 m b
86 01 35 m m
86 01 35 m b
86 01 18 m m
86 01 16 m b
86 01 14 m b
86 01 12 m b
86 01 10 m b
86 01 35 f b
86 01 35 f b
86 01 35 f b
86 01 25 f b
86 01 17 f m
86 01 6 f m
86 01 1 m m
86 01 1 f b
86 01 4/12 f b
86 01 20 f b
86 01 40 m b
86 01 15 m m

WARD, Berkley
86 01 60 m b
86 01 60 m b
86 01 40 m b
86 01 40 m b
86 01 25 m b
86 01 25 m b
86 01 16 m b
86 01 50 m b
86 01 50 f b
86 01 50 f b
86 01 25 f b

86 01 20 f m
CLARKE, Wm.
86 01 25 f m
BRAGG, Ann
86 01 24 f b
86 01 19 f b
86 01 16 m b
86 01 14 m b
WATERMAN, Simon
86 01 26 f m
86 01 11 f m
SPILMAN, John A.
86 01 31 f b
86 01 25 f m
86 01 23 f b
86 01 17 m m
86 01 14 f m
86 01 2 m m
PAYNE, Inman H.
86 01 60 m b
86 01 50 f b
86 01 40 f m
86 01 18 f b
86 01 12 f b
86 01 3 f b
HOWARD, Matilda
87 01 11 f b
MASSALETTIE, Lewis E.
87 01 20 f m
MOORE, Thomas L.
87 01 34 f m
87 01 11 m b
87 01 9 m b
87 01 6 m b
87 01 4 f b
87 01 2 m b
87 01 1/12 m b
JACKSON, Lucy
87 01 7 f b
TUTT, James M.
87 01 40 f b
87 01 10 f b
YATEMAN, George E.
87 01 55 m m
87 01 55 m b
87 01 45 m b
87 01 23 m b
87 01 18 m b
87 01 14 m b
87 01 12 m m
87 01 10 m m
87 01 45 f b
87 01 45 f m
87 01 25 f b
87 01 22 f b
87 01 4 f m
BAYLOR, Ann D.
87 01 45 f b
87 01 34 m b
87 01 12 f b
87 01 8 f b
87 01 6 f b
SPILMAN, Alexander H.
87 01 60 f b
87 01 15 f b
87 01 8 f b
PHILLIPS, Richard L.
87 01 27 f b
ROBBERTS, James
87 01 10 f b
SAUNDERS, Thomas E.
87 01 35 f b
87 01 11 f b
PAYNE, Rice W.
87 01 55 m b
87 01 35 f b
87 01 16 f b
87 01 14 f b
McCONKIE, Benj'n. H.
87 01 14 f b
CAMPBELL, Alexander
87 01 26 f b
87 01 16 f b
87 01 3 f b
87 01 2 m b
87 01 11 f b
87 01 8 m m
87 01 50 m b
87 01 50 m b
87 01 25 m b
87 01 23 m b
87 01 85 m b
87 01 70 f b
87 01 50 f b
87 01 6/12 m m
AYRES, Wm.

87	01	10	f	b
87	01	50	f	b
HORNER, Inman				
87	01	75	m	b
87	01	65	m	b
87	01	63	m	m
87	01	50	m	b
87	01	50	m	m
87	01	50	m	b
87	01	50	m	b
87	01	35	m	m
87	01	50	m	b
87	01	50	m	b
87	01	60	m	b
87	01	35	m	m
87	01	25	m	b
87	01	25	m	b
87	01	25	m	b
87	01	25	m	b
87	01	21	m	b
87	01	14	m	b
87	01	13	m	b
87	01	12	m	b
87	01	12	m	b
87	01	12	m	b
88	01	12	m	b
88	01	11	m	b
88	01	11	m	b
88	01	11	m	b
88	01	7	m	b
88	01	7	m	b
88	01	7	m	b
88	01	5	m	b
88	01	5	m	b
88	01	5	m	b
88	01	65	f	b
88	01	30	f	m
88	01	45	f	b
88	01	45	f	b
88	01	60	f	b
88	01	20	f	m
88	01	18	f	m
88	01	16	f	m
88	01	18	f	b
88	01	33	f	b
88	01	17	f	b
88	01	14	f	m
88	01	11	f	b
88	01	9	f	b
88	01	5	f	b
88	01	4	f	b
MONTJOY, John				
88	01	25	f	b
88	01	9	m	b
88	01	6	m	b
88	01	6/12	f	b
DRONE, Susan				
88	01	8	m	b
SMITH, G. W. F.				
88	01	35	m	b
88	01	22	m	b
88	01	22	m	b
88	01	24	m	b
88	01	24	m	b
88	01	27	m	b
88	01	4	m	b
88	01	6	m	b
88	01	42	f	b
88	01	43	f	b
88	01	21	f	b
88	01	17	f	b
88	01	12	f	b
88	01	1	f	b
88	01	1	m	b
BLACKWELL, James				
88	01	63	f	b
88	01	50	f	b
88	01	45	m	b
88	01	44	m	b
88	01	60	m	b
88	01	37	m	b
88	01	37	m	b
88	01	34	f	b
88	01	28	f	b
88	01	27	f	b
88	01	24	f	b
88	01	23	f	b
88	01	22	f	m
88	01	19	f	b
88	01	16	m	b
88	01	13	m	b
88	01	10	f	b
88	01	10	f	b
88	01	10	f	b
88	01	8	f	b
88	01	5	f	b

88	01	3	f	b
88	01	10	f	b
88	01	8	m	b
88	01	7	m	b
88	01	2	f	b
88	01	4/12	f	b
88	01	8	f	b
88	01	6	f	b
88	01	5	f	b
88	01	3	f	b
88	01	1/12	m	b
88	01	10	m	m
88	01	5	f	b
89	01	2	f	b
89	01	12	m	b

BLACKWELL, Joseph H.

89	01	52	m	b
89	01	30	m	b
89	01	22	m	b
89	01	19	m	b
89	01	17	m	b
89	01	60	m	b
89	01	25	f	b
89	01	21	f	b
89	01	13	f	b
89	01	6	m	b
89	01	4	f	b
89	01	1/12	f	b
89	01	5	f	b
89	01	4	f	b
89	01	3	f	b
89	01	1/12	m	b

JEFFRIES, Agatha

89	01	76	m	b
89	01	76	m	b
89	01	50	m	b
89	01	40	m	b
89	01	24	m	b
89	01	15	m	b
89	01	9	m	b
89	01	70	f	b
89	01	48	f	b
89	01	50	f	b
89	01	30	f	b
89	01	16	f	b
89	01	18	f	b
89	01	13	f	b
89	01	27	f	b

HORNER, Barbara

89	01	60	f	m
89	01	24	f	m
89	01	6	f	m
89	01	1	f	m

GASKINS, Mary E.

89	01	18	f	b
89	01	14	f	b
89	01	28	m	b
89	01	9	f	m

SMITH, J. Blackwell

89	01	36	m	b
89	01	32	f	b
89	01	28	m	b
89	01	25	m	b
89	01	21	f	b
89	01	14	f	b
89	01	14	f	b
89	01	14	f	b
89	01	14	m	b
89	01	9	f	b
89	01	8	m	b
89	01	7	f	b
89	01	4	m	b
89	01	2	m	b
89	01	35	f	b
89	01	2	m	b

SMITH, Wm. R.

89	01	71	m	b
89	01	71	m	b
89	01	55	m	b
89	01	56	m	b
89	01	46	m	b
89	01	33	m	b
89	01	32	m	b
89	01	34	m	b
89	01	32	m	b
89	01	33	m	b
89	01	24	m	b
89	01	26	m	b
89	01	16	m	b
89	01	14	m	b
89	01	3	m	b
89	01	62	f	b
89	01	62	f	b
89	01	57	f	b
89	01	57	f	b
89	01	36	f	b

89 01 23 f b
89 01 27? f b
90 01 18 f b
90 01 18 f b
90 01 17 f b
90 01 16 f b
90 01 7 f b
90 01 7 f m
90 01 3 f b
90 01 4 f m
90 01 3 f b
90 01 11 f b
90 01 12 f b
90 01 10 f b
90 01 58 f b

FLETCHER, Nancy
90 01 9 m b

UTTERBACK, French
90 01 50 f b
90 01 40 f b
90 01 28 f m
90 01 27 m b
90 01 26 f b
90 01 20 f b
90 01 18 m b
90 01 4 m m
90 01 4 m m
90 01 4 f m
90 01 4 f b
90 01 2 m b
90 01 2 m m
90 01 2 f b
90 01 7/12 f b
90 01 7/12 f b

BAILEY, Robert
90 01 12 f m

UTTERBACK, Armistead
90 01 60 m b
90 01 45 m b
90 01 27 m b
90 01 21 m b
90 01 18 m b
90 01 10 m b
90 01 6 m b
90 01 2 m b
90 01 30? m b
90 01 30 f b
90 01 25 f b
90 01 7 f b
90 01 2 f b
90 01 4/12 m b
90 01 55 m b
90 01 30 f b
90 01 8 m b
90 01 4 m b
90 01 1 f b

OGLEVIE, Elizabeth A.
90 01 50 f b
90 01 45 m b
90 01 35 m b
90 01 35 m b
90 01 20 m b
90 01 23 m m
90 01 12 m b
90 01 25 f b
90 01 7 f b
90 01 5 f b
90 01 4 m b
90 01 1 m b
90 01 17 f b
90 01 15 f b

UTTERBACK, Nathaniel
90 01 22 m b
90 01 18 m b
90 01 13 f b
90 01 23 f b
90 01 10 f b
90 01 9 m b
90 01 7 f m

CRAIG, Alexander S.
90 01 65 f b
90 01 66 f m
90 01 45 m m
90 01 25 m b
90 01 25 m b
90 01 22 f b
90 01 17 m b
90 01 15 m b
90 01 16 f b
91 01 12 m b
91 01 10 m b
91 01 9 f b
91 01 1 f b

NORMAN, Sally
91 01 70 m b
91 01 11 m b

WATERS, Sarah A.
91 01 9 f b
91 01 7 m b
91 01 5 m b
91 01 3 m b
CARTER, Presly
91 01 40 f b
91 01 22 m b
91 01 13 f b
91 01 12 f b
91 01 10 m b
DOUGLAS, Jacob
91 01 65 f b
91 01 50 f b
91 01 15 f b
91 01 10 f b
91 01 68 m b
91 01 30 m b
WARD, Berkley
91 01 60 m b
91 01 55 m b
91 01 55 m b
91 01 40 m b
91 01 35 m b
91 01 30 m b
91 01 30 m b
91 01 25 m b
91 01 25 m b
91 01 17 m b
91 01 50 m b
91 01 50 f b
91 01 10 m b
91 01 5 f b
91 01 30 f b
91 01 6 f b
91 01 5 f b
91 01 3 m b
91 01 3 f b
91 01 70 m b
91 01 60 f b
91 01 75 f b
SKINNER, Samuel
91 01 19 f b
LYLE, Thomas
91 01 50 f b
91 01 10 f b
HORD, Ambrose
91 01 60 f b
91 01 60 f b
91 01 18 f b
91 01 13 f b
91 01 11 f b
91 01 9 f b
91 01 9 f b
91 01 4 m b
91 01 2 m b
DESHIELDS, James
91 01 70 m b
91 01 60 m b
91 01 35 m b
91 01 22 m b
91 01 40 f b
91 01 32 f b
91 01 10 f b
FOOTE, Richard
91 01 76 f b
91 01 25 f b
91 01 19 f b
91 01 19 f m
91 01 17 f m
91 01 14 m b
91 01 70 m b
91 01 20 m b
91 01 15 m b
91 01 35 f b
91 01 11 f b
91 01 9 f b
91 01 6 m b
91 01 2 f b
91 01 1 f b
HORNER, Joseph
91 01 50 m m
91 01 50 f b
91 01 43? m b
92 01 46 m b
92 01 32 m b
92 01 26 m b
92 01 14 m b
92 01 9 m m
92 01 30 f m
92 01 26 f b
92 01 14 f fb
92 01 11 f m
92 01 6 m b
92 01 9 f m
92 01 7 m b

92 01 5 m b
92 01 3 m b
92 01 7 f b
BLACKWELL, Elizabeth
92 01 56 m b
92 01 48 f b
92 01 22 f b
92 01 14 m b
92 01 13 f b
92 01 11 f b
92 01 8 f b
92 01 1 m m
EDMONDS, Elias
92 01 66 m b
92 01 56 m b
92 01 40 m b
92 01 25 m b
92 01 20 m b
92 01 15 m b
92 01 12 m b
92 01 10 m m
92 01 7 m m
92 01 1 m b
92 01 60 f b
92 01 40 f b
92 01 35 f b
92 01 28 f b
92 01 15 f b
92 01 13 m b
92 01 13 f b
92 01 11 f b
92 01 9 f m
92 01 5 f b
92 01 5 f b
92 01 3 f m
92 01 7 f b
92 01 5 f b
92 01 65 m b
SUDDUTH, James
92 01 14 f b
BLACKWELL, John
92 01 63 f b
92 01 36 f b
92 01 34 f b
92 01 32 f b
92 01 27 f b
92 01 26 m b
92 01 22 m b
92 01 15 f m
92 01 14 f m
92 01 19 m b
92 01 9 m b
92 01 1 f b
92 01 1 f b
92 01 1 m b
92 01 15 m b
92 01 14 m b
92 01 9 m b
92 01 54 m b
92 01 52 m b
92 01 49 m b
SUTPHIN, Thomas
92 01 12 f m
HINSON, George W.
92 01 15 f b
92 01 9 m b
NORRIS, Thadeus
92 01 17 m b
92 01 14 f b
92 01 8 f b
92 01 6 f b
92 01 4 m b
92 01 28 f b
SAUNDERS, Judith
92 01 45 m b
92 01 35 m b
93 01 25 m b
93 01 24 m b
93 01 50 f b
93 01 40 f b
93 01 31 f b
93 01 20 f b
93 01 10 m b
93 01 10 m b
93 01 8 f b
93 01 7 m b
93 01 7 m b
93 01 6 m b
93 01 5 f b
93 01 2 m b
93 01 2 m b
93 01 2/12 f b
SMITH, Wm.
93 01 51 f b
93 01 40 m b
93 01 40 f b

93 01 40 f b
93 01 20 m b
93 01 20 m b
93 01 18 m b
93 01 16 m b
93 01 14 m b
93 01 12 f b
93 01 15 f b
93 01 10 m b
93 01 8 f b
93 01 6 f b
93 01 8 f b
93 01 3/12 f b
93 01 50 m b

THORNHILL, Winfield

93 01 18 f b
93 01 1/12 m b

SKINKER, James K.

93 01 45 f b
93 01 52 m b
93 01 20 m b
93 01 9 m b
93 01 8 m b
93 01 6 m b
93 01 4 m b
93 01 35 f b
93 01 17 m b
93 01 8 f b
93 01 5 f b
93 01 3 m b
93 01 18 f b
93 01 1 f b
93 01 13 m m
93 01 11 m b
93 01 7 m m
93 01 14 m b
93 01 67 m b
93 01 63 m b
93 01 48 m b
93 01 60 f b
93 01 24 m b
93 01 20 m b
93 01 27 m b
93 01 55 m b
93 01 55 m b
93 01 54 m b
93 01 54 m b
93 01 39 f b
93 01 17 f b
93 01 12 m m
93 01 10 m m
93 01 8 m m
93 01 5 f b
93 01 3 f b
93 01 38 f b
93 01 18 m b
93 01 14 f b
93 01 12 f b
93 01 8 m b
93 01 6 f b
93 01 3 m b
93 01 1 f b
93 01 34? f b
94 01 9 m m
94 01 5 m m
94 01 22 f b
94 01 5 m b
94 01 22 f b
94 01 3 f m
94 01 1 m b

TOMBLIN, Sarah

94 01 45 f b
94 01 40 f b
94 01 21 f b
94 01 20 f b
94 01 23 m m
94 01 19 m m
94 01 16 m b
94 01 8 f b
94 01 8 f b
94 01 4 f b
94 01 3 f b
94 01 2 f b

COCKRELL, Thomas

94 01 15 m b
94 01 5 m b

GLASCOCK, Henry

94 01 70 f b
94 01 20 m b
94 01 15 f b
94 01 13 m b
94 01 13 m b
94 01 9 m b
94 01 3 f b

TAYLOR, Armistead

94 01 25 f b

94 01 2 f b
SMITH, Robert E.
94 01 60 f b
94 01 58 m b
94 01 48 f b
94 01 35 f b
94 01 20 f b
94 01 21 m b
94 01 9 f b
94 01 7 m b
94 01 5 f b
94 01 3 m b
94 01 2 m b
94 01 1 m b
NEWHOUSE, Elias H.
94 01 9 m b
SMITH, Lycurgus
94 01 65 m b
94 01 62 f b
94 01 45 f b
94 01 19 f b
94 01 15 f b
94 01 8 m b
94 01 7 f b
94 01 6 m m
94 01 4 m b
94 01 3 m b
94 01 1 m b
SMITH, Wm. T.
94 01 55 m b
94 01 50 m b
94 01 24 f b
94 01 23 f b
94 01 19 m b
94 01 12 m b
94 01 10 f b
94 01 9 f b
94 01 6 f b
94 01 1 f b
94 01 7 f b
94 01 5 f b
94 01 2 f b
94 01 6 m b
94 01 4 f b
94 01 3 f b
94 01 5/12 f b
WELCH, Sylvester
94 01 55 m b
94 01 55 m b
94 01 55 m b
94 01 55 m b
94 01 36 m b
94 01 34 m b
94 01 34 m m
94 01 34 m b
94 01 50 m b
95 01 16 m b
95 01 14 m b
95 01 14 m b
95 01 6 m b
95 01 6 m m
95 01 6 m b
95 01 6 m b
95 01 6 m b
95 01 4 m b
95 01 4 m b
95 01 2 m b
95 01 2 m b
95 01 48 f b
95 01 30 f b
95 01 25 f b
95 01 25 f b
95 01 25 f b
95 01 12 f b
95 01 9 f m
95 01 8 f b
95 01 8 f b
95 01 6 f b
95 01 6 f b
95 01 4 f b
95 01 2 f b
95 01 3 f b
95 01 2 f b
95 01 3 f b
95 01 2 f b
FOLEY, James W.
95 01 68 m b
95 01 56 m b
95 01 47 f m
95 01 19 f b
95 01 17 f m
95 01 10 f b
95 01 6 m b
GARRISON, Wm.
95 01 28 m b
BEVERLY, Robert

95 01 33 m b
95 01 66 m b
95 01 31 m b
95 01 28 f b
95 01 28 f b
95 01 26 m b
95 01 24 f b
95 01 16 f b
95 01 16 m b
95 01 9 f b
95 01 6 m b
95 01 4 m b
95 01 3 m b
95 01 1 m b
95 01 6 m b
95 01 3 f b
95 01 1 m b
95 01 6/12 m b

FOLEY, Cecelia
95 01 60 m b
95 01 40 m b
95 01 39 f b
95 01 34 f b
95 01 19 f m
95 01 12 m m
95 01 10 m m
95 01 10 m b
95 01 8 m b
95 01 6 m b
95 01 4 m b
95 01 2 m b
95 01 9 f b
95 01 2 m b
95 01 32 m b
95 01 32 m b

BOSWELL, Thomas H.
95 01 85 f b
95 01 58 f b
95 01 42 f b
95 01 23 f b
95 01 18 m b
95 01 16 f b
95 01 14 m b
95 01 12 f b
95 01 10 m b
96 01 9 f b
96 01 6 f b
96 01 4 m b
96 01 2 m b
96 01 60 m b
96 01 60 m b
96 01 30 m b
96 01 25 m b

FORD, James F.
96 01 14 f b

COCHRAN, George B.
96 01 40 f b

DENEAL, Elizabeth D.
96 01 70 f b
96 01 12 f b
96 01 8 m b
96 01 4 m b

SMITH, Hedgeman
96 01 54 m b
96 01 50 m b
96 01 22 m b
96 01 21 m b
96 01 16 m b
96 01 55 f b
96 01 28 f m
96 01 23 f b
96 01 21 f b
96 01 16 f b
96 01 11 f b

LEWIS, James
96 01 70 m b
96 01 61 m b
96 01 50 m b
96 01 43 m b
96 01 35 m b
96 01 26 m b
96 01 25 m b
96 01 18 m b
96 01 13 m b
96 01 12 m b
96 01 10 m b
96 01 70 f b
96 01 60 f b
96 01 56 f b
96 01 38 f b
96 01 35 f b
96 01 28 f b
96 01 22 f b
96 01 18 f b
96 01 13 f b
96 01 12 f b

96 01 12 m b
96 01 10 f b
96 01 9 f b
96 01 9 m b
96 01 7 m b
96 01 7 f b
96 01 5 f b
96 01 5 f b
96 01 5 m b
96 01 5 m b
96 01 4 m b
96 01 4 m b
96 01 3 f b
96 01 3 f b

LEWIS, Henry M.

96 01 75 f b
96 01 65 m b
96 01 62 m b
96 01 60 f b
96 01 45 f b
96 01 38 m b
96 01 27 f b
96 01 26 m b
96 01 25 m b
96 01 24 f b
96 01 13 f b
96 01 9 f b
96 01 19 m b
96 01 9 m b
96 01 9 m b
96 01 8 m b
96 01 7 f b
96 01 6 f b

NALLS, Morgan W.

96 01 16 f b

SHACKELFORD, James B.

96 01 35 f b
97 01 22 m b
97 01 5 m m
97 01 3 f m

SHEARLY, James

97 01 16 f b

HUNTON, Elizabeth

97 01 46 f b
97 01 40 f m
97 01 50 m m
97 01 10 f b
97 01 7 m b
97 01 5 m b

HUNTON, Silas B.

97 01 55 m b
97 01 50 m b
97 01 35 f b
97 01 25 f b
97 01 14 m b
97 01 10 f b
97 01 8 m b
97 01 4 m b
97 01 3 m m
97 01 30 m m

MOREHEAD, Presly

97 01 45 f b
97 01 7 m b
97 01 45 m b
97 01 20 m b
97 01 20 m b
97 01 13 m b
97 01 14 f b

WEEKS, Joseph

97 01 6 f b
97 01 1 m b

GLASCOCK, Alfred

97 01 30 m b
97 01 25 m b
97 01 35 f b
97 01 12 f b
97 01 7 f b
97 01 4 f b
97 01 2 f b
97 01 1 m b

MILSTEAD, Henry

97 01 49 m b
97 01 17 f b

CHAPMAN, John

97 01 80 m b
97 01 60 m b
97 01 25 m b
97 01 22 m b
97 01 22 m b
97 01 20 m b
97 01 35 m b
97 01 60 f b
97 01 40 f b
97 01 25 f b
97 01 20 f b
97 01 35 f b

97 01 10 m m
97 01 8 f b
97 01 6 m b
97 01 5 m b
97 01 1 m b
97 01 6 f b

DULANY, Bladen
97 01 70 m b
97 01 58 m b
97 01 57 m b
97 01 57 m b
97 01 24 m b
97 01 23 m m
97 01 17 m b
97 01 15 m b
97 01 3 m m
97 01 2 m m
97 01 2 m b
97 01 5 f b
97 01 3 f b
97 01 4 f m
97 01 2 f m
97 01 4/12 f m
97 01 3/12 f b
97 01 3 f b
97 01 60 f b
97 01 50 f b
97 01 60 f b
97 01 20 f b
97 01 19 f b
98 01 17 f b
98 01 16 f m

KIRCHAVILLE, Sarah P.
98 01 23 m b
98 01 23 f b
98 01 10 f b
98 01 7 m b
98 01 5 f b
98 01 4 m b
98 01 2 f b

LEWIS, Elizabeth
98 01 65 f b
98 01 9 m b
98 01 12 m b

SAVAGE, Wm.
98 01 43 f b

HULET, Daniel
98 01 16 f b

DODD, George
98 01 15 m b

HUNTON, Edwin
98 01 50 m b
98 01 35 f b
98 01 30 m b
98 01 25 m b
98 01 16 f b
98 01 14 f b
98 01 7 m b
98 01 6 m m
98 01 5 f m

BROWN, Matilda
98 01 58 m b
98 01 49 m b
98 01 49 f b
98 01 40 m b
98 01 30 m b
98 01 30 m b
98 01 25 m b
98 01 19 m b
98 01 60 f m
98 01 15 m b
98 01 9 m b
98 01 13 f b
98 01 17 f b
98 01 37 f b
98 01 11 f b
98 01 7 f b
98 01 5 m b
98 01 3 m b
98 01 1 m b

HUNTON, Euphenia
98 01 40 f b
98 01 35 m b
98 01 32 m b
98 01 18 m b
98 01 17 f b
98 01 12 f b
98 01 10 m b

HUNTON, Wm. G.
98 01 39 m b
98 01 39 m b
98 01 27 f b
98 01 18 f m
98 01 9 f b
98 01 7 m b
98 01 42 m b

98 01 17 m b
98 01 11 f b

GRAYSON, Frederick W. S.
98 01 17 f m

HIXON, Mary
98 01 72 m b
98 01 44 f b
98 01 11 m b
98 01 9 f b
98 01 4 m b
98 01 10 f b

NALLS, John W.
98 01 12 f b

HAMPTON, Susan F.
98 01 14 f m
98 01 8 f m

BISE, Aaron
98 01 45 m b
98 01 25 f b
98 01 21 f b
98 01 16 f b
98 01 16 f b
98 01 8 m b
98 01 6 m b
98 01 5 m m
98 01 3 m b
98 01 3 m b
98 01 3 f b
99 01 3 m b
99 01 3/12 f b
99 01 80 m b

KLIPSTINE, Philip A.
99 01 60 m b
99 01 18 m b
99 01 28 f b
99 01 5 m b
99 01 1 f b
99 01 90 f b
99 01 35 f b
99 01 12 f b
99 01 3 m b
99 01 1 m b

BASEY, Edmond
99 01 22 f b
99 01 7 f m
99 01 4 m b
99 01 3 m b
99 01 1 m b

SINCLAR, Wm. D.
99 01 25 m b
99 01 40 f b
99 01 9 m b
99 01 6 m b
99 01 1 f b
99 01 12 f b

RYAN, Malinda
99 01 26 f b

CLAGGET, Julia
99 01 60 f m
99 01 22 f m
99 01 7 f m
99 01 2 m m

FRANCIS, Wm.
99 01 35 f b
99 01 14 m m

FRANCIS, Andrew
99 01 13 m m
99 01 12 m b
99 01 10 m b

JOHNSON, Moses
99 01 29 m b
99 01 23 f b
99 01 19 f b
99 01 12 f b
9 01 12 m b
99 01 12 m b
99 01 5 f b
99 01 3 f b
99 01 7/12 f b

TOLER, Philip
99 01 52 f b
99 01 20 f b
99 01 2 m m
99 01 1 f b

THOMAS, John H.
99 01 28 f b
99 01 5 f b
99 01 3 m b

FRENCH, James
99 01 30 f b

EDMONDS, Alexander
99 01 28 m b
99 01 25 m b
99 01 25 m b
99 01 25 f m
99 01 25 f b

99 01 4 f m
99 01 4 f m
99 01 3 m m
99 01 1 f m
99 01 7 m b
99 01 4 f b
99 01 1 m b
99 01 85 f m
99 01 75 f b
CARNELL, John
99 01 20 m b
99 01 18 f b
CLAGGET, James A.
99 01 30 f b
99 01 40 m b
99 01 15 m b
99 01 9 f m
99 01 7 m b
99 01 6 m b
99 01 5 f b
99 01 2 m b
DRUMMOND, Leanora
99 01 28 f b
99 01 15 m b
99 01 14 m m
99 01 8 f b
99 01 7 f m
99 01 5 f b
100 01 4/12 m b
SEARS, Campbell
100 01 18 m m
SYDNOR, John M.
100 01 12 f b
HUNTON, Thomas E.
100 01 65 f b
100 01 57 m b
100 01 55 m b
100 01 55 m b
100 01 35 m m
100 01 34 f b
100 01 30 f m
100 01 18 f b
100 01 6 m b
100 01 5 m m
100 01 17 m b
LERACH, Jessee W.
100 01 26 f b
100 01 14 f b
100 01 15 m b
100 01 7 f m
100 01 1 m b
HUNTON, Charles
100 01 48 m b
100 01 63 m b
100 01 63 f b
100 01 42 m b
100 01 37 m b
100 01 33 f b
100 01 26 f b
100 01 23 m b
100 01 30 m b
100 01 35 f b
100 01 25 m b
100 01 16 m b
100 01 14 f b
100 01 12 m b
100 01 10 f b
100 01 9 m b
100 01 6 f b
100 01 5 f b
100 01 4 f b
100 01 3 f b
100 01 2 f b
100 01 1 f b
100 01 1 f b
100 01 43 m b
BARTLETT, John
100 01 15 f b
GARNER, Elizabeth
100 01 7 f b
SYDNOR, John M.
100 01 12 f b
MOORE, John
100 01 9 m b
100 01 7 f b
100 01 5 f b
100 01 2 f b
HOE, Hanson
100 01 14 f b
100 01 15 m b
JEFFRIES, Willis
100 01 40 f m
100 01 12 m b
100 01 11 m b
100 01 6 f m
WEAVER, Wm. P.

100 01 80 f b
100 01 50 f b
100 01 50 m m
100 01 40 m b
100 01 17 m b
100 01 17 m b
100 01 35 f m
100 01 35 f b
100 01 40 f b
100 01 20 f b
100 01 35 m b
100 01 10 m b
100 01 5 f b
100 01 1 m b
100 01 1 f b
100 01 11 f b
100 01 10 m m

WARDER, Thornberry
100 01 60 m b
100 01 43 m b
100 01 22 f b
100 01 17 m b
100 01 2 f b
100 01 3/12 m b

SUTHARD, James
100 01 65 f b

PRESTON, Benj'n.
101 01 35 f b
101 01 8 f b
101 01 6 m b
101 01 3 m b

FITZHUGH, Martha S.
101 01 65 m b
101 01 29 f m
101 01 29 f b
101 01 23 m b
101 01 20 m b
101 01 19 f b
101 01 15 m b
101 01 15 m b
101 01 14 f m
101 01 12 m b
101 01 12 f b
101 01 14 m b
101 01 7 f b
101 01 3 m b
101 01 1 m b
101 01 4 m m

FITZHUGH, Lucy B.
101 01 60 m b
101 01 48 m b
101 01 63 m b
101 01 57 f b
101 01 56 f b
101 01 45 f b
101 01 19 f b
101 01 12 m m
101 01 13 f m

OGG, John B.
101 01 54 f b

COLVIN, Haywood
101 01 60 m m
101 01 30 f b
101 01 28 f b
101 01 13 f b
101 01 11 m b
101 01 8 f b
101 01 8 m b
101 01 6 m b
101 01 6 f b

WILKINS, Thomas
101 01 54 f b
101 01 30 f b
101 01 15 f b
101 01 12 f b
101 01 10 m b
101 01 7 f b
101 01 2 m b

STONE, Richard
101 01 45 f b
101 01 29 m b
101 01 22 f b
101 01 18 f b
101 01 16 m b
101 01 13 f b
101 01 10 f b
101 01 4 m b
101 01 1 f b
101 01 55 f b

HOE, Rice
101 01 60 m b
101 01 50 f b
101 01 48 m b
101 01 25 m b
101 01 23 m b
101 01 20 m b

101 01 21 f b
101 01 21 f b
101 01 13 f b
101 01 12 m b
101 01 12 m b
101 01 11 m b
101 01 11 m b
101 01 16 f b
101 01 2 m b
101 01 2 m b
101 01 1/12 f b
101 01 1/12 f b
CLANAHAM, Elizabeth
101 01 40 f b
101 01 3 m m
MANUEL, John W.
101 01 15 f b
STOVEN, Charles J.
101 01 85 f b
101 01 23 f b
101 01 23 f b
102 01 20 f b
102 01 17 f m
102 01 18 f b
102 01 9 f b
102 01 4 m b
102 01 3 f b
102 01 1 m b
102 01 2 f b
102 01 65 m b
102 01 50 m b
102 01 30 m b
102 01 27 m b
102 01 24 m b
102 01 20 m b
102 01 17 m b
102 01 16 m b
102 01 14 m m
102 01 13 m b
102 01 9 m b
LAWS, Newton
102 01 37 f b
102 01 21 m b
102 01 20 m b
102 01 12 m b
102 01 3 m b
102 01 15 f b
CRUMP, Reuben M.
102 01 25 f m
102 01 2 f b
102 01 1 f b
102 01 10 f b
McCARTY, Wm.
102 01 25 m b
102 01 21 m b
102 01 16 m b
102 01 18 f b
102 01 12 f b
102 01 10 m b
102 01 7 f b
102 01 8 f b
102 01 6/12 m b
CATLETT, Samuel
102 01 60 m b
102 01 33 m b
102 01 50 f b
102 01 30 f m
102 01 25 f b
102 01 20 f b
102 01 13 m m
102 01 12 f b
102 01 7 f b
102 01 5 f b
102 01 5 f b
102 01 1 f b
102 01 1 f b
102 01 1 f b
WEEDEN, Robert
102 01 45 f b
102 01 17 m b
102 01 8 f b
ELLIOT [ELLICOT], Willis
102 01 30 f b
102 01 19 f b
102 01 6 f b
102 01 3 f b
MANUEL, Francis
102 01 13 m b
102 01 8 f b
COLVIN, Richard
102 01 30 f m
102 01 16 m m
102 01 13 f b
102 01 7 f b
102 01 5 m b
102 01 1 f m

102 01 60 f b
102 01 17 f b
102 01 8 f b

COLVIN, Wm.
102 01 30 m b
102 01 16 f b
102 01 11 f b

PARMER, Joseph
102 01 50 m b
102 01 30 m b
102 01 30 m b
102 01 25 m b
102 01 25 m b
102 01 40 f b
102 01 35 f b
103 01 45 f b
103 01 30 f m
103 01 25 f b
103 01 18 f b
103 01 15 f b
103 01 14 f b
103 01 60 f b
103 01 9 f b
103 01 10 f b
103 01 8 f b
103 01 7 f b
103 01 8 m b
103 01 6 f b
103 01 5 m b
103 01 4 m b

COLVIN, James
103 01 25 f b
103 01 15 m b
103 01 8 m m
103 01 3 m b
103 01 5/12 f b

FOWKE, Thomas W.
103 01 40 f b
103 01 24 m b
103 01 7 f m
103 01 7 f b
103 01 5 m b
103 01 3 f b
103 01 2 f b
103 01 1 m b

SUTHARD, Wm.
103 01 45 f b *
* blind

HUFFMAN, Wm.
103 01 22 f b

BREWER, Wm.
103 01 8 m b
103 01 5 m b
103 01 1 f b
103 01 30 f b

SMALLWOOD, George W.
103 01 70 f b

PAGE, Wm. H.
103 01 60 f b
103 01 45 f b
103 01 25 f b
103 01 22 f b
103 01 20 f b
103 01 4 f b
103 01 2 f b
103 01 4 f m
103 01 6/12 f m
103 01 21 m b
103 01 20 m m
103 01 28 m b
103 01 40 m b
103 01 12 m b
103 01 12 f b
103 01 2 m m

KEYS, John H.
103 01 80 f b
103 01 12 m b

KING, Richard B.
103 01 12 f b

WEAVER, Samuel
103 01 80 m m
103 01 45 m b
103 01 45 f b
103 01 35 m m
103 01 35 f b
103 01 30 m m
103 01 27 m b
103 01 27 m m
103 01 27 f b
103 01 12 m b
103 01 3 m b
103 01 1 f b

BUTLER, Nathaniel B.
103 01 80 f b
103 01 60 f b
103 01 60 m b

103 01 45 m b
103 01 45 m b
103 01 40 f b
103 01 30 f b
103 01 12 f b
103 01 ? ? m
103 01 10 m b
103 01 8 m b
103 01 6 m m
103 01 6 f b
103 01 5 m b
104 01 3 f b
104 01 3 f b
104 01 1 f b
104 01 1 f b

WEAVER, Richard A.
104 01 17 f m
104 01 16 f b
104 01 15 m m
104 01 4 f b

SIMPSON, John
104 01 8 m b

PETERS, Mary
104 01 39 f b
104 01 33 m b
104 01 25 f b
104 01 20 f b
104 01 15 f b
104 01 12 m b
104 01 11 m b
104 01 10 f b
104 01 9 f b
104 01 9 m b
104 01 8 m b
104 01 8 f b
104 01 4 f b
104 01 4 m b
104 01 4 f b
104 01 2 m b
104 01 1 f b
104 01 4/12 f b

SHUMATE, Bailey
104 01 70 m b
104 01 60 f b
104 01 45 m b
104 01 35 f b
104 01 34 f b
104 01 34 m b
104 01 29 m b
104 01 23 m b
104 01 28 m b
104 01 21 f b
104 01 17 m m
104 01 17 m b
104 01 16 m b
104 01 17 f b
104 01 9 m b
104 01 7 m b
104 01 1 f b

GAINS, Philip P.
104 01 13 f b

WEAVER, Elizabeth
104 01 70 f b
104 01 62 f b
104 01 56 f b
104 01 30 f b
104 01 25 f m
104 01 30 m b
104 01 27 m b
104 01 26 m b
104 01 12 m b
104 01 14 f m
104 01 10 m b
104 01 9 m m
104 01 10 f b
104 01 8 f b
104 01 7 f b
104 01 7 f m
104 01 4 m m
104 01 4 m m
104 01 4 m m
104 01 1 m m
104 01 5 m b
104 01 3 f b
104 01 56 m b

REDD, Sarah C.
104 01 25 f b
104 01 23 m b
104 01 19 f b
104 01 10 m b
104 01 10 m b
104 01 3 m b
104 01 1 f b
104 01 31 m b

REDD, Dodridge
104 01 60 m b

104 01 60 m b
104 01 30 f b
104 01 30 f b
105 01 30 f b
105 01 10 f b
105 01 10 f b
105 01 7 m b
105 01 7 m b
105 01 4 m b

REDD, Joseph
105 01 65 f b
105 01 30 m b
105 01 24 f b
105 01 14 m b
105 01 11 m b
105 01 3 f b

WALLER, Lewis
105 01 60 m b
105 01 48 m b
105 01 48 m b
105 01 50 m b
105 01 37 m b
105 01 48 f b
105 01 30 m b
105 01 30 f b
105 01 12 f m
105 01 8 f b
105 01 5 f b
105 01 3 m m
105 01 4 m b
105 01 28 m b
105 01 55 m b

GEORGE, Bernard
105 01 57 f b
105 01 24 f b
105 01 17 f b
105 01 1 m b *
* idiotic
105 01 4 m b
105 01 40 f b
105 01 25 f m
105 01 6 m b
105 01 5 m b
105 01 3 m b
105 01 8 m m
105 01 6 m m
105 01 4 m m
105 01 65 f b
105 01 14 f b
105 01 14 m b
105 01 8 f b
105 01 6 f b
105 01 4 f b
105 01 18 f b
105 01 4 f b
105 01 2 m b
105 01 16 f b
105 01 45 f b
105 01 20 m b
105 01 18 m b
105 01 14 m b
105 01 10 m b
105 01 8 f b
105 01 6 f b
105 01 4 f b
105 01 50 f b
105 01 30 f b
105 01 25 f b
105 01 14 m b
105 01 35 f b
105 01 18 m b
105 01 10 m b
105 01 8 m b
105 01 6 m b
105 01 2 m b
105 01 40 m b

McUNTY, Alexander
105 01 20 m b
105 01 2 f m
105 01 1 m m

ELICOTT, Thomas
105 01 20 f b
105 01 16 f b

GAINS, Richard H.
105 01 70 f b
105 01 48 f b
105 01 45 m b
105 01 41 m b
105 01 30 m m
105 01 26 f b
106 01 19 f b
106 01 17 f b
106 01 16 f b
106 01 15 f b
106 01 11 f b
106 01 2 m b

106 01 2 m b
106 01 1 f b
HOE, Howser
106 01 85 f b
106 01 58 f m
106 01 53 f b
106 01 50 m b
106 01 47 m b
106 01 44 f b
106 01 44 f b
106 01 38 m b
106 01 37 m b
106 01 36 f b
106 01 27 m b
106 01 27 m b
106 01 26 m b
106 01 26 m m
106 01 26 m m
106 01 22 m b
106 01 22 m b
106 01 21 m b
106 01 15 m b
106 01 26 f b
106 01 11 m m
106 01 10 m b
106 01 3 f b
106 01 2 f b
106 01 3 f b
106 01 2 f b
106 01 13 m b
106 01 10 f m
SHUMATE, Thomas
106 01 50 m b
106 01 50 f b
106 01 17 f b
CARICO, Josiah
106 01 55 m b
McCORMACK, Wm.
106 01 18 f b
PAGE, John
106 01 33 f b
106 01 24 m b
106 01 17 f m
106 01 11 f b
106 01 9 f b
106 01 9 m b
106 01 7 m b
106 01 4 m b
106 01 2 m b
BALCH, Thomas B.
106 01 55 m b
106 01 40 m b
106 01 45 f b
106 01 7 f b
106 01 25 f m
106 01 4 m m
106 01 32 f b
106 01 7 m b
106 01 5 f b
106 01 3 f b
106 01 1 m b
FITZHUGH, Thomas L.
106 01 25 f m
106 01 20 f m
106 01 16 m b
106 01 4 m m
106 01 2 m m
106 01 2 m m
106 01 1 m m
106 01 15 m b
FRANCIS, Robert H.
106 01 20 f b
106 01 15 m b
106 01 10 m b
GRAY, Sarah
106 01 60 f m
106 01 55 f b
106 01 55 m b
106 01 10 f b
CHICHESTER, Fanny
106 01 50 f b
106 01 11 m b
106 01 10 f b
106 01 9 f b
107 01 60 m b
MITCHELL, Charlotte N.
107 01 60 m b
107 01 25 f b
107 01 23 f b
107 01 18 m b
107 01 13 f b
107 01 12 f b
107 01 12 m b
107 01 9 m m
107 01 2 m m
JEFFRIE, James

107 01 12 m b
WILLIAMSON, Sarah
107 01 93 f b
107 01 50 m b
107 01 38 f m
107 01 28 f b
107 01 22 m b
107 01 24 f b
107 01 10 m b
107 01 9 m b
107 01 8 f b
107 01 7 f b
107 01 7 f b
107 01 6 f b
107 01 6 f m
107 01 3 m b
107 01 3 f b
107 01 2 f b
107 01 2 f b
107 01 1 m b
107 01 1 f b
WALLER, Elizabeth
107 01 80 f b
107 01 65 m b
107 01 50 f b
107 01 38 f b
107 01 34 f b
107 01 31 f b
107 01 27 m b
107 01 25 m b
107 01 18 f b
107 01 16 f b
107 01 16 m b
107 01 14 f b
107 01 12 f b
107 01 11 m b
107 01 11 m b
107 01 10 f b
107 01 10 m b
107 01 9 f b
107 01 9 f b
107 01 8 m b
107 01 7 f b
107 01 7 f b
107 01 7 m b
107 01 6 m b
107 01 4 f b
107 01 1 m b
107 01 1 m b
107 01 3/12 f b
107 01 5 f b
BAYLISS, John T.
107 01 60 f b
107 01 24 m b
PAGE, Wm. S.
107 01 60 m b
107 01 45 m b
107 01 28 f b
107 01 23 f b
107 01 15 f b
107 01 14 m b
107 01 10 m b
107 01 7 f b
107 01 6 m b
107 01 5 m b
107 01 5 m b
107 01 4 m b
107 01 8/12 m b
107 01 2/12 f b
PAYNE, Nancy
107 01 62 m m
107 01 45 f m
107 01 35 f b
107 01 35 f b
107 01 40 m m
108 01 38 m m
108 01 25 f m
108 01 20 f b
108 01 12 f b
108 01 9 m m
108 01 9 m b
108 01 7 f m
108 01 6 f b
108 01 2 m b
108 01 6 m m
108 01 3 m b
108 01 1 f b
108 01 3/12 f b
108 01 1/12 f b
108 01 1/12 f b
O'REAR, Thomas D.
108 01 70 m b
108 01 50 m b
108 01 44 f b
108 01 35 f b
108 01 15 m b

108	01	12	m	b
108	01	6	m	b
108	01	4	m	b
108	01	3	f	b
108	01	2	m	b
108	01	2	f	b
108	01	7	f	b
108	01	5	m	b
108	01	3	f	b

ROLLS, Sally

108	01	20	f	b
108	01	10	m	b
108	01	3	m	b
108	01	2/12	m	b

McCOY, John

108	01	45	f	m
108	01	24	m	b
108	01	18	f	b
108	01	10	m	b
108	01	5	m	m
108	01	1	m	b

SMITH, Wilford A.

108	01	60	m	b
108	01	40	f	b
108	01	38	f	b
108	01	30	m	b
108	01	28	f	b
108	01	22	f	b
108	01	20	m	b
108	01	13	m	b
108	01	13	m	b
108	01	12	f	b
108	01	10	f	b
108	01	5	m	b
108	01	2	m	b
108	01	1	m	b
108	01	1	f	b
108	01	1	f	b
108	01	6/12	m	b

FRENCH, James dec'd.

108	01	75	m	b
108	01	60	f	b
108	01	47	f	b
108	01	44	m	b
108	01	38	m	b
108	01	34	m	b
108	01	30	f	b
108	01	28	f	b
108	01	20	f	b
108	01	18	f	b
108	01	17	f	b
108	01	14	f	b
108	01	14	m	b
108	01	12	f	b
108	01	11	m	b
108	01	8	m	b
108	01	9	f	b
108	01	8	f	b
108	01	8	m	b
108	01	7	f	b
108	01	6	m	b
108	01	7	f	b
108	01	4	f	b
108	01	1	m	b
109	01	4	f	b
109	01	5	m	b
109	01	4	m	b
109	01	1	f	b
109	01	2/12	f	b

MCCOY, Delia

109	01	95	f	b
109	01	70	f	b
109	01	55	m	b
109	01	35	m	b
109	01	20	f	b
109	01	19	m	b
109	01	16	f	m
109	01	15	f	m
109	01	15	f	b
109	01	8	m	m
109	01	7	m	m
109	01	5	f	m
109	01	2	f	b

ARINGTON, John W.

109	01	53	m	b
109	01	30	f	b
109	01	7	f	b
109	01	6	m	b
109	01	1	f	b

CUMMINS, John

109	01	45	f	b
109	01	26	m	b
109	01	24	f	b
109	01	2	m	b
109	01	13	m	b

THARPE, Thomas

109	01	48	f	b
109	01	58	m	b
MOXLEY, James J.				
109	01	29	f	m
109	01	7	f	m
109	01	4	m	m
BROOKES, Wm.				
109	01	10	f	b
HILL, Fanny				
109	01	35	f	m
109	01	18	m	b
109	01	18	m	b
109	01	12	m	b
HARDING, Angeline				
109	01	45	f	b
109	01	11	f	b
109	01	11	f	m
109	01	50	m	b
109	01	18	m	b
109	01	17	f	b
TAYLOR, Simon T.				
109	01	50	f	b
109	01	19	m	b
109	01	19	f	b
109	01	14	m	b
CUMMINS, Bethelena				
109	01	25	m	b
109	01	30	f	b
109	01	20	m	b
109	01	19	m	b
109	01	6	f	b
109	01	4	m	b
109	01	2	m	b
109	01	4/12	f	b
PAYNE, Robert				
109	01	40	m	b
109	01	35	m	b
109	01	35	m	b
109	01	30	f	b
109	01	30	f	b
109	01	20	m	b
109	01	20	f	b
109	01	17	m	b
109	01	12	f	b
109	01	11	f	b
109	01	11	f	b
109	01	9	m	b
109	01	6	f	b
109	01	5	m	b
109	01	5	m	b
109	01	3	m	b
109	01	2	f	b
109	01	2	f	b
COWNE, Thomas W.				
109	01	50	f	b
109	01	40	f	b
109	01	19	m	b
109	01	13	m	b
109	01	13	m	b
109	01	10	m	b
110	01	6	f	b
110	01	5	m	b
110	01	5	m	b
110	01	2	f	b
COX, Hugh				
110	01	29	m	b
110	01	21	m	b
110	01	18	f	b
110	01	15	m	b
110	01	10	m	b
110	01	4	m	b
WALTON, Melville N.				
110	01	28	m	b
110	01	25	m	b
110	01	33	f	b
110	01	54	m	b
110	01	11	f	b
110	01	11	f	b
110	01	10	f	b
110	01	8	m	b
110	01	7	f	b
110	01	4	f	b
110	01	3	f	b
110	01	2	m	b
110	01	2	f	b
HANSBOROUGH David				
110	01	55	m	b
110	01	48	m	b
110	01	45	f	b
110	01	28	f	b
110	01	26	f	b
110	01	23	f	b
110	01	18	f	m
110	01	10	m	m
110	01	5	m	m
110	01	5	m	b

110 01 3 f m
BAXTER, Wm.
110 01 15 f b
COMBS, Peggy
110 01 62 m b
110 01 62 m b
110 01 62 m b
110 01 42 m b
110 01 16 m b
110 01 36 m m
110 01 26 f b
110 01 30 f b
110 01 26 f b
110 01 22 m b
110 01 15 m b
110 01 30 f m
110 01 25 m b
110 01 19 f b
110 01 16 m b
110 01 9 m b
110 01 19 m b
110 01 9 m m
110 01 5 m b
110 01 8 f m
110 01 19 m m
110 01 10 m m
110 01 4 m b
110 01 4 f b
110 01 2 f b
WALLER, Fanny
110 01 60 m b
110 01 60 m b
110 01 45 f b
110 01 40 f b
110 01 20 f b
110 01 15 m b
110 01 12 m b
110 01 8 f b
110 01 6 f b
110 01 4 m b
110 01 5 m b
110 01 2 f b
LUCKETT, Salina
110 01 50 m b
110 01 49 f b
110 01 28 f b
110 01 14 m b
110 01 12 f b
110 01 10 m b
110 01 8 m b
110 01 7 m b
111 01 5 f b
111 01 3 f b
111 01 5/12 m b
TULLOSS, Wm. H.
111 01 14 m b
TULLOSS, Joseph R.
111 01 28 f m
111 01 10 m m
111 01 7 f b
111 01 4 f m
111 01 1 m m
BOTTS, Thornton
111 01 50 f b
111 01 40 m b
111 01 29 m b
111 01 30 m b
111 01 32 f m
111 01 18 m b
111 01 11 f m
111 01 8 f b
111 01 5 f b
111 01 4 m b
111 01 2 f b
MOSEE, Gibson
111 01 18 f b
111 01 13 m b
PETERS, Henry
111 01 68 m b
111 01 70 f b
111 01 50 m b
111 01 48 m b
111 01 45 f b
111 01 35 f b
111 01 25 f b
111 01 23 m b
111 01 20 m b
111 01 14 m b
111 01 12 m b
111 01 12 m b
111 01 8 m b
111 01 10 f b
111 01 14 f b
111 01 12 f b
111 01 6 f b
111 01 3 f b

111 01 6 f b
111 01 4 m b
111 01 2 m b
111 01 3 m b
111 01 1 m b
111 01 12 m b

GEORGE, Joseph
111 01 45 f b
111 01 23 f b
111 01 23 m b
111 01 21 m b
111 01 18 f b
111 01 18 f b
111 01 17 m b
111 01 10 f b
111 01 10 f b
111 01 3 f b
111 01 3 f b
111 01 1 m b

BUTLER, W. H.
111 01 52 f b
111 01 28 f b
111 01 27 f b
111 01 24 m b
111 01 20 m b
111 01 18 m b
111 01 15 f b
111 01 12 f b
111 01 12 m b
111 01 6 f b
111 01 8 m b
111 01 7 f b
111 01 5 m b
111 01 2 f b
111 01 5/12 f b
111 01 8 f m
111 01 5 f m
111 01 1 f m

REED, John
111 01 40 m b

PETERS, Jessee
111 01 60 f b
111 01 53? m b
111 01 46 f b
112 01 37 f b
112 01 31 f b
112 01 28 f b
112 01 26 m b
112 01 19 f b
112 01 17 f b
112 01 10 m b
112 01 15 m b
112 01 15 m b
112 01 11 m b
112 01 9 m b
112 01 9 f b
112 01 8 f b
112 01 8 m b
112 01 8 f b
112 01 8 m b
112 01 5 m b
112 01 5 f b
112 01 5 m b
112 01 4 m b
112 01 3 f b
112 01 3 m b
112 01 2 m b
112 01 2 f b
112 01 1 f b

GEORGE, Mary
112 01 50 m b
112 01 50 f b
112 01 50 m b
112 01 45 m b
112 01 30 m b
112 01 16 m b
112 01 17 f b
112 01 30 f b
112 01 30 f b
112 01 12 m b
112 01 8 m b
112 01 6 m b
112 01 4 m b
112 01 2 f b
112 01 1 f b

EUSTUS, Louisa
112 01 59 f b
112 01 32 f b
112 01 22 f b
112 01 18 m b
112 01 17 m b
112 01 10 m m
112 01 6 f b
112 01 6 f b
112 01 5 m b
112 01 4 f b

112 01 2 m b
112 01 2/12 m b
112 01 2/12 f b
112 01 22 m b *
* idiotic

BUTLER, Edward
112 01 75 m b
112 01 75 f b
112 01 75 f b
112 01 40 m b
112 01 35 m b
112 01 34 f b
112 01 23 m b
112 01 21 m b
112 01 19 f b
112 01 13 m b
112 01 12 m b
112 01 8 m b
112 01 7 m b
112 01 5 m b
112 01 2 f b

OLLIVER, Reason H.
112 01 40 f b
112 01 35 f b
112 01 18 f b
112 01 13 f b
112 01 10 m b
112 01 9 m b
112 01 6 m b
112 01 6 f b
112 01 4 m b
112 01 4 m b
112 01 2 m b
113 01 3/12 m b
113 01 4 m b

HERNDON, Wm.
113 01 44 f b
113 01 23 f b
113 01 19 m b
113 01 16 f b
113 01 9 f b
113 01 6 m m
113 01 3 f b
113 01 3 m b *
* fugitive

HERNDON, Haywood
113 01 8 m b

McCORMACK, Stephen
113 01 50 m b
113 01 16 m b
113 01 24 f b

EDMONDS, Sarah B.
113 01 45 f b
113 01 40 m b
113 01 29 f b
113 01 23 f b
113 01 20 m b
113 01 19 f b
113 01 11 f b
113 01 11 f b
113 01 7 m b
113 01 5 m b
113 01 4 f m
113 01 7 f b
113 01 5 f b
113 01 3 m b
113 01 1 f m

GRAY, Nathaniel N.
113 01 35 f b
113 01 32 m b
113 01 20 m b
113 01 8 m b
113 01 6 m b
113 01 4 f b
113 01 2/12 f b

CLEGGET, George A.
113 01 12 f b

WHITE, Redmond F.
113 01 57 m m
113 01 45 f b
113 01 13 f b
113 01 5 f b
113 01 3 f b
113 01 2 f b
113 01 2/12 f b

CHICHESTER, Eliza
113 01 60 f m
113 01 50 f b
113 01 22 m b
113 01 60 m b
113 01 21 m m
113 01 11 m b
113 01 9 m b
113 01 8 m m

EDMONDS, Thomas
113 01 50 m b

113 01 49 f b
113 01 26 f b
113 01 14 f b
113 01 13 m b
113 01 13 f b
113 01 4 m b
113 01 2 f b
113 01 9/12 f b
113 01 9/12 m m

FITZHUGH, Giles
113 01 40 m b
113 01 38 f b
113 01 30 m b
113 01 20 m b
113 01 12 m b
113 01 8 m b
113 01 4 f b
113 01 3 f b
113 01 1 m b
113 01 17 f b
113 01 17 f b
113 01 8? m b
113 01 4 f b
113 01 2 m b
113 01 3 f b
113 01 16 f b
113 01 17 f b

PILCHER, Armistead T.
113 01 17 f b
114 01 6 m b

MARTIN, Henry C.
114 01 50 f b
114 01 24 f b
114 01 19 m b
114 01 12 f b

WEAVER, Joseph
114 01 45 m b
114 01 30 m b
114 01 30 m b
114 01 25 m b
114 01 20 m b
114 01 20 f b
114 01 25 f b
114 01 15 m b
114 01 12 m b
114 01 12 m b
114 01 20 f b
114 01 7 m b
114 01 4 m b
114 01 4 m b
114 01 3 m b
114 01 2 f b
114 01 2 f b

LATHAM, Thomas N.
114 01 45 f b
114 01 40 f b
114 01 25 m b
114 01 25 m b
114 01 17 m b
114 01 14 m b
114 01 14 m b
114 01 12 f b
114 01 3 m b
114 01 3 m b
114 01 2 f b
114 01 1 f b

WEAVER, Joseph Jnr.
114 01 60 m b
114 01 40 m b
114 01 40 m b
114 01 30 m b
114 01 18 m b
114 01 16 m b
114 01 16 m m
114 01 14 m m
114 01 10 m m
114 01 7 m b
114 01 5 m b
114 01 5 m b
114 01 40 f b
114 01 38 f b
114 01 35 f b
114 01 10 f b
114 01 15 f b
114 01 8 f b
114 01 8 f b
114 01 2 f b
114 01 9 f b
114 01 4 f b

JOLLIFF, Wm. H.
114 01 50 f b
114 01 30 m b
114 01 12 m b
114 01 1 m m

WEAVER, Wm. S.
114 01 53 f b

114 01 48 m b
114 01 30 m b
114 01 18 f b
114 01 18 f b
114 01 12 f b
114 01 1 f b
114 01 25 m b

PETERS, Isaac
114 01 27 f b
114 01 21 m b
114 01 20 m b
114 01 19 f b
114 01 14 m b
114 01 12 f b
114 01 12 f m
114 01 8 m b
114 01 5 m b
114 01 3 f b

MORROW, James
114 01 65 m b
114 01 40 f b
115 01 38 f b
115 01 20 f b
115 01 19 f b
115 01 16 m b
115 01 10 f b
115 01 8 m b
115 01 6 m b
115 01 3 f b
115 01 3 f b
115 01 1 f b
115 01 3/12 f b
115 01 10 f b

WEAVER, Charles A.
115 01 61 f b
115 01 32 f b
115 01 42 f b
115 01 25 f b
115 01 21 m b
115 01 8 f b
115 01 8 f b
115 01 6 m b
115 01 4 f b
115 01 4 f b
115 01 1 f b

BUTLER, Townsend
115 01 13 m b

PILCHER, Alexander S.
115 01 60 m b
115 01 35 m b
115 01 33 f b
115 01 13 m b
115 01 12 f b
115 01 11 f b
115 01 9 m b
115 01 7 m b
115 01 6 f b
115 01 3 f b

BOWER, Alexander P.
115 01 21 m b
115 01 30 f b
115 01 19 m b
115 01 16 f b
115 01 14 f b
115 01 10 f b
115 01 2 f b

BUTLER, Sarah
115 01 65 m b
115 01 65 m b
115 01 35 m b
115 01 37 f b
115 01 30 f b
115 01 20 f b
115 01 14 f b
115 01 13 m b
115 01 12 m b
115 01 11 m b
115 01 10 m b
115 01 8 m b
115 01 8 f b
115 01 6 f b
115 01 4 f b
115 01 3 f b
115 01 1/12 f b

GREEN, Elizabeth
115 01 30 f b
115 01 7 f b
115 01 6 f b
115 01 12 f b

GEORGE, Weeden
115 01 26 m b
115 01 23 m b
115 01 30 f b
115 01 24 f b
115 01 13 m b
115 01 12 m b

115 01 8 m b
115 01 8 f b
115 01 7 f b
115 01 5 m b
115 01 4 m b
COOPER, Jonathan
115 01 80 m b
115 01 50 f b
115 01 44 f b
115 01 42 m b
115 01 35 m b
115 01 24 f m
115 01 20 f m
116 01 16 f m
116 01 14 m b
116 01 14 m b
116 01 10 m b
116 01 9 m b
116 01 9 m m
116 01 1 m b
116 01 5 m b
116 01 2 f b
116 01 6/12 m b
116 01 6/12 m m
116 01 6/12 f b
116 01 1 m b
116 01 1 m m
116 01 12 m b
116 01 26 f b
BAILY, James W.
116 01 60 m b
116 01 50 f b
116 01 40 m b
116 01 36 m b
116 01 50 f m
116 01 50 f b
116 01 50 f b
116 01 24 f m
116 01 15 m m
116 01 13 f m
116 01 10 m b
116 01 8 m b
116 01 5 f b
116 01 1/12 m b
116 01 8 m b
116 01 7 m b
116 01 2 f m
116 01 14 f b
EMBRY, George
116 01 12 f b
HELM, Lina
116 01 95 f b
116 01 70 f b *
* blind
116 01 40 f b
116 01 40 f b
116 01 25 f b
116 01 35 m b
116 01 35 m m
116 01 22 m b
116 01 14 f b
116 01 12 f b
116 01 11 m b
116 01 10 f b
116 01 4 m b
116 01 3 m b
ENSOR, Wm. R.
116 01 80 f b
116 01 60 f b
KANE, Davenport
116 01 88 f b
SHUMATE, Wm.
116 01 60 f b
116 01 35 f b
116 01 11 m b
116 01 10 f b
ROLLS, Harvey
116 01 60 m b
116 01 35 f b
116 01 16 f b
116 01 7 f b
116 01 2 m b
116 01 1 f b
LOMAS, Thomas M.
116 01 45 m b
116 01 24 m b
116 01 14 f b
RANDOLPH, Robert L.
116 01 52 m b
116 01 49 m b
116 01 54 f b
116 01 43 f b
116 01 41 f b
116 01 36 m b
116 01 56 m b
116 01 28 f m

116 01 43 f m
116 01 29 f b
116 01 26 f b
116 01 22 f b
116 01 21 m m
116 01 20 m b
116 01 18 f b
117 01 13 f b
117 01 12 f b
117 01 11 m b
117 01 10 m b
117 01 10 m m
117 01 10 m m
117 01 8 m b
117 01 8 m m
117 01 7 f b
117 01 6 m b
117 01 4 f m
117 01 4 m b
117 01 4 f b
117 01 4 f b
117 01 3 f m
117 01 2 m b
117 01 8/12 m b
117 01 5/12 m m
117 01 26 f m
117 01 25 m b
117 01 24 m b
117 01 22 m b
117 01 19 f b
117 01 17 f b
117 01 15 m b
117 01 15 m b
117 01 9 m b
117 01 9 f b
117 01 8 f b
117 01 7 f b
117 01 7 f m
117 01 6 f b
117 01 5 m m
117 01 5 m b
117 01 4 f b
117 01 3 m m
117 01 2 m b
117 01 1 m b

CHILDS, Wm.

117 01 80 f b
117 01 56 m m
117 01 48 m b
117 01 31 m b
117 01 28 m b
117 01 20 m b
117 01 43 f b
117 01 27 f b
117 01 24 f b
117 01 14 f b
117 01 12 m b
117 01 10 f b
117 01 7 m b
117 01 7 m b
117 01 4 f b
117 01 2 m b
117 01 2 m b

HOLDER, Taliafero

117 01 19 m m
117 01 19 m b
117 01 19 f b
117 01 24 f m
117 01 8 f m
117 01 4 f b
117 01 2 m b

HOLTSCLAW, George W.

117 01 55 m b
117 01 20 f b

MILIGAN, Elizabeth

117 01 35 f b
117 01 32 f m
117 01 25 f b
117 01 25 m b

JONES, Amos

117 01 12 f b

TOMPKINS, Robert R.

117 01 25 m b
117 01 23 f b
117 01 43 m b
117 01 22 f b
117 01 20 f b
117 01 20? f b
117 01 14 m b
117 01 9 m b
117 01 6 m b
117 01 7 m b
117 01 5 m b
118 01 5 f b
118 01 2 f b

JEFFRIES, John

118 01 60 f b
118 01 36 f m
118 01 10 m b
118 01 5 m m
118 01 3 m b

SMITH, Walter
118 01 50 m b
118 01 50 f b

BAGGET, James W.
118 01 20 m b

PORTER, John
118 01 32 m b
118 01 17 f b
118 01 17 m b
118 01 14 f b
118 01 10 m b
118 01 6 f b
118 01 22 f b
118 01 4 f b
118 01 2 f b
118 01 1 f b

LEWIS, Frederick
118 01 68 m b
118 01 60 m b
118 01 45 f b
118 01 18 m b
118 01 14 m b
118 01 10 m b
118 01 7 m b

EDWARDS, Bushrod
118 01 19 f b

RICKETTS, John
118 01 40 f b
118 01 13 f b
118 01 12 m b
118 01 10 m b
118 01 9 f b
118 01 9 f b
118 01 5 f b
118 01 61 m b

BRIGGS, Robert
118 01 40 f b
118 01 24 f b
118 01 18 m m
118 01 31 m b
118 01 11 m b

WHITE, John L.
118 01 65 m b
118 01 65 m b
118 01 45 f b
118 01 35 m m
118 01 30 m b
118 01 28 m b
118 01 21 m b
118 01 20 f b
118 01 16 m b
118 01 14 m b
118 01 4 f b
118 01 2 f b
118 01 25 f m

VOWELLS, Newton
118 01 65 f b
118 01 45 f b
118 01 50 m b
118 01 30 m b
118 01 29 m b
118 01 24 m b
118 01 18 m b
118 01 10 f b
118 01 8 f b
118 01 3 m b

BERKLEY, Daniel
118 01 13 f b

DIGGS, Humphrey D.
118 01 12 f b

FLETCHER, Stephen S.
118 01 7 m b

JOHNSON, Horace
118 01 25 f b
118 01 40 m b
118 01 30 m b
118 01 25 m b

HULET, Richard K.
118 01 16 f m

FURR, Abraham
118 01 17 f b

JEFFRIES, Esther S.
118 01 28 m b
118 01 25 m b
118 01 24 f b
118 01 19 f b
118 01 15 m b
118 01 12 m b
118 01 6 m b
119 01 4 f b
119 01 2 f b

119 01 5/12 f b
119 01 45 f b
MARSHALL, John
119 01 68 f b
119 01 72 f b
119 01 48 f b
119 01 45 m b
119 01 44 m b
119 01 30 m b
119 01 28 m b
119 01 56 f m
119 01 26 m b
119 01 45 m b
119 01 27 f b
119 01 16 f b
119 01 14 m b
119 01 15 m b
119 01 12 m m
119 01 9 f b
119 01 10 m b
119 01 8 f b
119 01 18 f b
119 01 22 f b
119 01 3 m b
119 01 1 f m
119 01 3 m b
119 01 2 f b
119 01 1 f b
119 01 65 m b
119 01 26 m b
WOLFE, Andrew Junr.
119 01 35 f b
119 01 25 m b
119 01 16 f b
119 01 12 m b
119 01 10 m m
119 01 8 f b
119 01 6 f b
119 01 4 m b
119 01 6/12 f b
119 01 20 f b
LOVE, George
119 01 70 f b
119 01 38 f b
119 01 33 f b
119 01 32 f b
119 01 31 f b
119 01 22 f b
119 01 40 f b
119 01 16 f b
119 01 10 f b
119 01 10 f b
119 01 5 f b
119 01 7 f b
119 01 5 f b
119 01 3 f b
119 01 2 f b
119 01 1 f b
119 01 72 m b
119 01 32 m b
119 01 28 m b
119 01 26 m b
119 01 25 m b
119 01 23 m b
119 01 20 m b
119 01 16 m b
119 01 14 m b
119 01 14 m b
119 01 72 m b
119 01 12 m b
119 01 12 m b
119 01 9 m b
119 01 9 m b
119 01 7 m b
119 01 4 m b
119 01 4 m b
119 01 11 m b
119 01 7 m b
119 01 6 m b
119 01 4 m b
119 01 2 m b
120 01 5/12 m b
120 01 81 m b
LOVE, Mary
120 01 63 f b
120 01 55 m b
120 01 45 m b
120 01 32 m b
JONES, Thomas
120 01 75 m b
120 01 27 m b
120 01 18 m b
MITCHELL, John
120 01 70 m b
120 01 38 m b
120 01 51 f b

120 01 17 f b
120 01 15 m b
120 01 20 m b
MITCHELL, John Junr.
120 01 48 f b
120 01 28 m b
120 01 25 f b
120 01 18 f b
120 01 11 m b
120 01 10 f b
120 01 7 m b
120 01 8 f b
120 01 5 f b
120 01 6 m b
120 01 4 f b
120 01 3 f b
120 01 2/12 f b
120 01 1/12 f b
HALE, Olevia D.
120 01 70 f b
120 01 45 f b
120 01 42 m m
120 01 37 f b
120 01 19 m b
120 01 17 f b
120 01 17 m b
120 01 15 f b
120 01 11 f b
120 01 10 m b *
* blind
120 01 10 f b
120 01 9 m b
120 01 8 m b
120 01 8 m b
120 01 6 m b
120 01 2 f b
SCANLAND, John
120 01 42 f b
120 01 23 m b
120 01 5 f m
120 01 4/12 m b
HUTCHINSON, Wm. F.
120 01 65 f b
SWARTS, Wm.
120 01 52 m b
120 01 44 f b
120 01 30 m b
120 01 24 m b
120 01 21 m b
120 01 17 m b
120 01 22 f b
120 01 9 m m
120 01 6 m b
120 01 6 f b
120 01 3 m b
120 01 21 f b
SKINNER, James
120 01 40 f b
120 01 30 m b
120 01 28 m b
120 01 22 m m
120 01 22 m b
120 01 18 f b
120 01 15 m b
120 01 6 f b
120 01 3 m b
120 01 1 f b
TORRISON, Samuel
120 01 60 m b
SAMPSELL, Henry G.
120 01 75 f b
RECTOR, Joseph T.
120 01 40 m b
120 01 40 f b
120 01 30 m b
120 01 17 m m
120 01 6 f b
120 01 4 f b
121 01 3 m b
121 01 1 m b
CHINN, Charles E.
121 01 42 f b
121 01 35 m b
121 01 16 m b
121 01 12 f b
121 01 10 f b
121 01 8 f b
121 01 6 m b
121 01 3 f b
CHINN, Elijah
121 01 28 m b
121 01 19 m m
121 01 35 f m
121 01 7 m m
121 01 3 f m
121 01 2/12 m m

RECTOR, Samuel
121 01 50 m m
121 01 21 m b
121 01 30 f b
121 01 13 m b
121 01 11 m b
121 01 9 f b
121 01 7 f b
121 01 5 f b
121 01 3 f b
121 01 1/12 m b
121 01 15 f b
JOHNSON, Thomas
121 01 10 f b
HATCHER, Gurley R.
121 01 55 m b
121 01 55 f b
121 01 18 f b
121 01 18 m b
121 01 16 f b
121 01 14 m b
121 01 10 f b
121 01 30 m m
GIBSON, Nelson
121 01 26 f m
121 01 22 m b
121 01 16 m b
121 01 14 f m
121 01 10 f m
121 01 5 f m
121 01 3 m m
FLETCHER, Wm. Junr.
121 01 46 m b
121 01 33 m b
121 01 24 m b
121 01 20 f b
121 01 21 f b
121 01 20 m b
121 01 15 m b
121 01 14 m b
121 01 15 f b
LAKE, Ludwell
121 01 9 f b
121 01 24 m b
121 01 20 f b
121 01 12 m b
121 01 12 m b
121 01 8 f b
121 01 6 f b
121 01 3 m b
121 01 22 m b
121 01 19 m m
121 01 16 f b
RECTOR, Caleb
121 01 65 f b
121 01 40 m b
121 01 20 f b
121 01 22 m b
121 01 17 f b
121 01 15 f b
121 01 11 f b
121 01 11 m b
DAVIS, Hamilton J.
121 01 50 f b
121 01 4 f m
TEBBS, Samuel J.
121 01 60 f b
121 01 65 f b
121 01 57 m b
121 01 46 m b
121 01 46 m b
121 01 45 m b
121 01 42 f b
122 01 33 m m
122 01 30 f b
122 01 28 f b
122 01 28 f b
122 01 40 m m
122 01 19 m b
122 01 19 m b
122 01 17 f b
122 01 14 f m
122 01 12 m b
122 01 11 f b
122 01 9 m b
122 01 5 f b
122 01 6 f b
122 01 4 f b
122 01 3 f b
122 01 2 m b
TRIPLETT, Thomas
122 01 60 f b
122 01 40 m b
122 01 60 m b
122 01 45 m b
122 01 40 m b

122 01 42 m b
122 01 20 f b
122 01 9 f b
122 01 7 f b
122 01 33 f b
122 01 31 m b
122 01 26 f b
122 01 8 m b
122 01 7 f b
122 01 3 m b
122 01 1 m b

REID, Alfred

122 01 30 f b
122 01 33 m b
122 01 27 m b
122 01 21 m b
122 01 19 m b
122 01 15 m b
122 01 13 m b
122 01 9 f b
122 01 9 m m
122 01 7 f b
122 01 6 f b
122 01 5 m b
122 01 3 f b
122 01 2 f b
122 01 14 m b
122 01 26 f b

WHEELER, Jackson

122 01 14 f b

BYRNE, Uriah

122 01 74 f b
122 01 46 f b
122 01 23 m m
122 01 12 m b

BYRNE, James

122 01 14 m b

DORSEY, Daniel E.

122 01 54 f b
122 01 48 m b
122 01 30 m b
122 01 10 f b
122 01 7 f b

POWELL, Peyton

122 01 75 f b
122 01 35 f b
122 01 2 f b

HUTCHERSON, Joseph A.

122 01 42 m b
122 01 20 m b
122 01 16 f b
122 01 10 f b

GLASCOCK, Edith

122 01 70 f b
122 01 45 m b
122 01 10 m b

HITT, Wm.

122 01 7 m b

GASKINS, Wm. E.

122 01 40 m b
122 01 38 m b
122 01 38 f b
122 01 28 f b
122 01 10 m b
122 01 6 m b
122 01 73 m b

PAYNE, Richards

122 01 60 m b
122 01 50 m b
123 01 40 m b
123 01 21 m b
123 01 45 f b
123 01 35 f b
123 01 10 m b
123 01 10 m b
123 01 8 f b
123 01 6 f b
123 01 7 m b
123 01 4 m b

KEMPER, John

123 01 12 f m

PADGET, Robert

123 01 40 m b
123 01 12 f b
123 01 12 m m

FITZGERALD, James

123 01 72 m b
123 01 65 m b
123 01 48 m b
123 01 44 m b
123 01 43 m b
123 01 41 m b
123 01 53 m b
123 01 54 m m
123 01 42 m b
123 01 21 m b

123 01 31 m m
123 01 20 m b
123 01 21 m b
123 01 26 m b
123 01 16 m b
123 01 15 m b
123 01 35 m b
123 01 49 m b
123 01 35 m b
123 01 46 m b
123 01 22 m b
123 01 38 f b
123 01 36 f b
123 01 26 f b
123 01 29 f b
123 01 37 f b
123 01 19 m b
123 01 40 f b
123 01 29 f m
123 01 19 f m
123 01 29 f b
123 01 21 f b
123 01 28 f b
123 01 62 f b
123 01 52 f b
123 01 5 m b
123 01 1 m b
123 01 10 m b
123 01 3 m b
123 01 2 m b
123 01 12 m b
123 01 11 m b
123 01 9 m b
123 01 8 m b
123 01 2 m b
123 01 1 m b
123 01 4 m b
123 01 8 m b
123 01 10 m b
123 01 8 m b
123 01 5 m b
123 01 10 f b
123 01 8 f b
123 01 7 f b
123 01 1 f b
123 01 12 f b
123 01 12 f b
123 01 10 f b
123 01 9 f b
123 01 6 f b
123 01 14 f b
123 01 9 f b
123 01 5 f b
123 01 3 f b
123 01 7 f b
123 01 5 f b
124 01 7 f b
124 01 2 f b
124 01 4/12 f b
124 01 6 f m
124 01 4 f b
124 01 2 f b

CRITINDEN, Polly
124 01 20 m b
124 01 15 f m
124 01 10 m b

HELM, Richard P.
124 01 9 m b
124 01 7 f b
124 01 10 f b

HELM, Joanna
124 01 65 m b
124 01 40 f b
124 01 9 f b
124 01 4 m b
124 01 3 f b
124 01 25 m b
124 01 65 f b

JONES, Wm. A.
124 01 29 f m
124 01 1 m b
124 01 13 f b
124 01 5 f b

SMITH, Wm. J.
124 01 50 f b
124 01 19 m b

OLLIVER, Richard T.
124 01 30 f m
124 01 18 m b
124 01 13 f b
124 01 10 f b
124 01 4 f b
124 01 1 f b

EMBRY, Garnet
124 01 30 f b

STEPHENS, Briant

124 01 50 f b
124 01 45 m b
124 01 16 m b
124 01 13 m b
124 01 10 f b

VOTZ, John
124 01 45 f b

SWARTZ, John
124 01 10 f b

TULLOSS, Richard
124 01 50 f b
124 01 12 f b

HICKERSON, Wm. E.
124 01 40 m b
124 01 23 f b
124 01 19 f b
124 01 12 m b
124 01 9 m b
124 01 8 f b
124 01 3 f b
124 01 1 f b
124 01 1 f b

SMITH, Wm. A.
124 01 25 f b
124 01 18 f b
124 01 12 f b
124 01 8 m b
124 01 4 m b
124 01 2 m b

THOMPSON, Joseph
124 01 70 f b
124 01 65 f b
124 01 40 m b
124 01 40 m b
124 01 28 m b
124 01 20 m b
124 01 18 m b
124 01 19 m b
124 01 20 m b
124 01 18 m b
124 01 19 m b
124 01 20 f b
124 01 19 f b
124 01 18 f b
124 01 19 f b
124 01 10 m b
124 01 9 m b
124 01 10 m b
124 01 10 m b
124 01 9 m b
124 01 2 f b
124 01 3 m b
124 01 3 m b
124 01 2 m b
125 01 2 m b
125 01 1 m b
125 01 1 m b

HUME, Elizabeth
125 01 45 m b
125 01 50 m b
125 01 50 f b
125 01 35 f b
125 01 20 f b
125 01 8 m b
125 01 6 f b
125 01 4 f b
125 01 3 m b
125 01 1 m b

STEPHENS, Alexander
125 01 30 m b
125 01 8 f b

THOMPSON, Mary A.
125 01 60 m b
125 01 29 m b
125 01 27 m b
125 01 16 f b
125 01 10 m b
125 01 7 f b

HEFFLIN, George
125 01 30 f b
125 01 11 f b

ESKRIDGE, Rodham
125 01 60 f b
125 01 50 f b
125 01 45 m b
125 01 24 f b
125 01 23 f b
125 01 24 f b
125 01 24 f b
125 01 10 f m
125 01 4 f b
125 01 11 f b
125 01 2 f b
125 01 10 m b
125 01 1 f b
125 01 1 f b

125 01 1 f b
125 01 22 m b
125 01 2 f b

PRIMM, John

125 01 59 f b
125 01 53 f b
125 01 32 f b
125 01 31 m b
125 01 29 m b
125 01 13 f b
125 01 12 m b
125 01 10 m b
125 01 9 m b
125 01 7 f b
125 01 6 m b
125 01 4 m b
125 01 3 m b
125 01 2 f b
125 01 1 f b

HELM, John G.

125 01 65 m b
125 01 45 f b
125 01 22 m b
125 01 11 f b
125 01 4 m b
125 01 4 f b
125 01 2 f b

GORDON, Alexander

125 01 45 f b
125 01 43 f m
125 01 32 m b
125 01 28 m b
125 01 15 m b
125 01 13 f b
125 01 11 m b
125 01 11 m m
125 01 9 m m
125 01 8 m b
125 01 6 f b
125 01 5 f b
125 01 5 f m
125 01 4 m b
125 01 1 f b
125 01 38 f b

LEARY, John

125 01 39 m b
125 01 30 m b
126 01 33 f b
126 01 15 m b
126 01 8 f m
126 01 11 m m
126 01 7 f m
126 01 5 f m
126 01 3 f m
126 01 1 m m

BRONAUGH, John T.

126 01 60 m b
126 01 45 f b
126 01 24 f b
126 01 22 m b
126 01 45 m b
126 01 14 m b
126 01 14 f b
126 01 8 m b
126 01 2 f b

HORNER, Benj'n F.

126 01 3 m m
126 01 43 m b
126 01 35 m b
126 01 3/12 f m
126 01 30 f b

CARTER, Richard H.

126 01 44 m b
126 01 34 m b
126 01 26 m b
126 01 22 m m
126 01 17 m b
126 01 16 m b
126 01 14 m b
126 01 11 m b
126 01 10 m b
126 01 5 m b
126 01 7 f b
126 01 31 f b
126 01 31 f m
126 01 11 f b
126 01 8 f b
126 01 6 f b
126 01 3 f b
126 01 2 f b
126 01 2 f b
126 01 16 f m

POLLARD, Elizabeth

126 01 72 m b
126 01 52 f b
126 01 10 f b

126	01	7	f	b

DOWELL, John C.

126	01	22	f	b
126	01	14	m	b
126	01	6	f	b
126	01	3	f	b
126	01	1/12	f	b

INDEX

Index

D

G

N

R

S

Y

Heritage Books by Patricia B. Duncan:

1850 Fairfax County and Loudoun County, Virginia Slave Schedule

1850 Fauquier County, Virginia Slave Schedule

1860 Loudoun County, Virginia Slave Schedule

Clarke County, Virginia Death Register, 1853–1896, with Birth Records, 1855–1856, Entered on Death Register

Clarke County, Virginia Marriages, 1836–1886

Clarke County, Virginia Marriages, 1887–1925

Clarke County, Virginia Will Book Abstracts: Books A–I (1836–1904) and 1A–3C (1841–1913)

Fairfax County, Virginia Birth Register, 1853–1879

Fairfax County, Virginia Birth Register, 1880–1896

Fauquier County, Virginia, Birth Register, 1853–1880

Fauquier County, Virginia, Birth Register, 1881–1896

Fauquier County, Virginia, Marriage Register, 1854–1882

Fauquier County, Virginia, Marriage Register, 1883–1906

Fauquier County, Virginia Death Register, 1853–1896

Hunterdon County, New Jersey 1895 State Census, Part I: Alexandria–Junction

Hunterdon County, New Jersey 1895 State Census, Part II: Kingwood–West Amwell

Genealogical Abstracts from The Lambertville Press, *Lambertville, New Jersey: 4 November 1858 (Vol. 1, Number 1) to 30 October 1861 (Vol. 3, Number 155)*

Genealogical Abstracts from The Democratic Mirror *and* The Mirror, *1857–1879, Loudoun County, Virginia*

Genealogical Abstracts from The Mirror, *1880–1890, Loudoun County, Virginia*

Genealogical Abstracts from The Mirror, *1891–1899, Loudoun County, Virginia*

Genealogical Abstracts from The Mirror, *1900–1919, Loudoun County, Virginia*

Genealogical Abstracts from The Telephone, *1881–1888, Loudoun County, Virginia*

Genealogical Abstracts from The Telephone, *1889–1896, Loudoun County, Virginia*

Jefferson County, [West] Virginia Death Register, 1853–1880

Jefferson County, West Virginia Death Register, 1881–1903

Jefferson County, Virginia 1802–1813 Personal Property Tax Lists

Jefferson County, Virginia 1814–1824 Personal Property Tax Lists

Jefferson County, Virginia 1825–1841 Personal Property Tax Lists

Jefferson County, Virginia (later West Virginia), Will Book Abstracts, Volumes 1 and 2, 1801–1816
Patricia B. Duncan and Elizabeth R. Frain

1810–1840 Loudoun County, Virginia Federal Population Census Index

1860 Loudoun County, Virginia Federal Population Census Index

1870 Loudoun County, Virginia Federal Population Census Index

Abstracts from Loudoun County, Virginia Guardian Accounts: Books A–H, 1759–1904

Abstracts of Loudoun County, Virginia Register of Free Negroes, 1844–1861

Index to Loudoun County, Virginia Land Deed Books A–Z, 1757–1800

Index to Loudoun County, Virginia Land Deed Books 2A–2M, 1800–1810

Index to Loudoun County, Virginia Land Deed Books 2N–2U, 1811–1817

Index to Loudoun County, Virginia Land Deed Books 2V–3D, 1817–1822

Index to Loudoun County, Virginia Land Deed Books 3E–3M, 1822–1826

Index to Loudoun County, Virginia Land Deed Books 3N–3V, 1826–1831

Index to Loudoun County, Virginia Land Deed Books 3W–4D, 1831–1835

Index to Loudoun County, Virginia Land Deed Books 4E–4N, 1835–1840

Index to Loudoun County, Virginia Land Deed Books 4O–4V, 1840–1846

Index to Loudoun County, Virginia Land Tax Lists, 1782–1802

Index to Loudoun County, Virginia Land Tax Lists, 1803–1817

Loudoun County, Virginia Birth Register, 1853–1879

Loudoun County, Virginia Birth Register, 1880–1896

Loudoun County, Virginia Clerks Probate Records Book 1 (1904–1921) and Book 2 (1922–1938)

Loudoun County, Virginia Criminal Indictments: 1801–1843

Loudoun County, Virginia Marriages after 1850: Volume 1, 1851–1880
Patricia B. Duncan and Elizabeth R. Frain

Loudoun County, Virginia Marriages after 1850: Volume II, 1881–1900
Patricia B. Duncan and Elizabeth R. Frain

Loudoun County, Virginia Partially Proven Deeds

Loudoun County, Virginia Office Judgments: 1786–1794 and 1794–1806

Loudoun County, Virginia Office Judgments: 1806–1817 and 1817–1822

Loudoun County, Virginia Office Judgments: 1822–1827 and 1827–1835

Loudoun County, Virginia Office Judgments: 1835–1842 and 1842–1847

Loudoun County, Virginia 1800–1810 Personal Property Taxes

Loudoun County, Virginia 1826–1834 Personal Property Taxes

Loudoun County, Virginia Will Book Abstracts, Books A–Z, Dec. 1757–Jun. 1841

Loudoun County, Virginia Will Book Abstracts, Books 2A–3C, Jun. 1841–Dec. 1879 and Superior Court Books A and B, 1810–1888

Loudoun County, Virginia Will Book Index, 1757–1946

Genealogical Abstracts from The Brunswick Herald, *Brunswick, Maryland: Mar. 6 1891–Dec. 28 1894*

Genealogical Abstracts from The Brunswick Herald, *Brunswick, Maryland: Jan. 4 1895–Dec. 30 1898*

Genealogical Abstracts from The Brunswick Herald, *Brunswick, Maryland: Jan. 6 1899–Dec. 26 1902*

Genealogical Abstracts from The Brunswick Herald, *Brunswick, Maryland: Jan. 2 1903–June 29 1906*

Genealogical Abstracts from The Brunswick Herald, *Brunswick, Maryland: July 6 1906–Feb. 25 1910*

Marriage and Death Notices from the Genius of Liberty, *1817–1843*
Marty Hiatt, Ann Hennings and Patricia B. Duncan

CD: *Articles and Advertisements from Leesburg, Virginia Newspapers The Washingtonian (6 Feb 1810–16 Jul 1811) and The Genius of Liberty (11 Jan 1817–20 May 1843)*

CD: *Index to Fairfax County, Virginia Personal Property Tax Lists, 1782–1850*

CD: *Fairfax County, Virginia Minute/Order Books, 1749–1808*

CD: *Loudoun County, Virginia Minute/Order Books: January 1804 to October 1820*

CD: *Loudoun County, Virginia Order Books A-I, 1757–1786*

CD: *Loudoun County, Virginia Order Books K-W, 1787–1803*

CD: *Loudoun County, Virginia Personal Property Tax List, 1782–1850*

www.ingramcontent.com/pod-product-compliance
Lightning Source LLC
LaVergne TN
LVHW020633100826
845148LV00012B/2175

* 9 7 8 1 5 8 5 4 9 8 1 9 2 *